Egypt

This book has three main themes. The first part is designed to give some insight into the life of the archaeologist in Egypt, who gets on to a dig, what the work is like, and the physical conditions under which work is carried out. The second part concerns the daily life of the ancient Egyptians as it can be reconstructed from the finds made by archaeologists. The third section deals with individual finds and excavations and is designed to show how important an individual find can be in reconstructing the history of a country, even though the object concerned may be of little intrinsic value or artistic merit. In this section the author, who has had the good fortune to spend three seasons with Professor W. B. Emery on the Egypt Exploration Society's excavations at Sakkara, shows how the archaeologist sometimes finds it necessary to turn detective in order to piece together a puzzle of the past.

THE YOUNG ARCHAEOLOGIST BOOKS
Edited by Robin Place, MA, FSA

Egypt

ANNE MILLARD

WITH AN INTRODUCTION BY
PROFESSOR W. B. EMERY

Rupert Hart-Davis Educational Publications   London

Granada Publishing Limited
First published in Great Britain 1971
by Rupert Hart-Davis Educational Publications
3 Upper James Street, London, WIR 4BP

ISBN 0 298 79121 8
Set in Photon Times 12 pt. by
Richard Clay (The Chaucer Press), Ltd., Bungay, Suffolk
and printed in Great Britain by
Fletcher & Son, Ltd., Norwich, Norfolk

Contents

List of Illustrations

Foreword

I feel that it is particularly important that authors of books for young people should have first-hand experience of their material. Miss Anne Millard is an Egyptologist who has worked with me on the excavations at Sakkara. In this book she describes very vividly the conditions under which we work in this lovely country, and points out the different ways in which discoveries from excavations can contribute to our knowledge of the Ancient Egyptians. I am pleased to see some of our unsolved problems laid frankly before the reader, who should, after finishing this absorbing book, have a good idea of the aims of Egyptologists at the present time.

W. B. EMERY MBE, MA, D. LIT., FBA, FSA

Field Director Egypt Exploration Society excavations at Sakkara

The Pronunciation of Ancient Egyptian Names

This book is not designed to cover the transliteration and translation of ancient Egyptian hieroglyphs. The reader may find it useful, however, to know roughly how to pronounce some of the names that will be found in the text. Ancient Egyptian was written without vowels, so these have to be added by philologists. Different authorities, however, tend to use different vowels, so the reader must not be upset if he finds a word spelled in different ways in different books. Egyptians had several letters for which there are no exact English equivalents. Thus, the Egyptian letter $\underline{h}$ is usually written *kh* in English and is to be pronounced rather like the *ch* in the Scottish word "loch".

Tutankhamen – Toot-an"ch"-amen.

Akhenaten – A"ch"-n-at-n.

Hetepheres – Hett-ep-herries.

Menes – Meanies.

Thebes – Theebs.

Nefertiti – Neffer-tea-ty.

Tiy – Tea.

Amenhotep – Amen-hoe-tep.

Ramesses – Ram-essies.

Deir – Dear.

Abydos – Abb-eye-doss.

Hatshepsut – Hat-shepp-soot.

Tuthmosis – Tuth-moe-siss.

CHAPTER ONE

Tourists, Tomb Robbers, and Archaeologists

In the beautiful land that borders the river Nile, the ancient Egyptians and their god-kings, the Pharaohs, produced one of the earliest and the greatest civilizations of the Ancient World. At one time they ruled the Near East from the Euphrates River in the north to the Fifth Cataract of the Nile in the south, and their culture survived, relatively unchanged, for over three thousand years of recorded history.

"Over three thousand years of recorded history." It takes a great effort of the imagination to put into proper perspective the centuries that separate us from the very first Pharaohs. One thousand years ago England was still ruled by the Anglo-Saxons and Leif Ericson had not yet sailed to America. Two thousand years ago Jesus of Nazareth had not been born; the Romans ruled the known world, and Cleopatra, the last independent ruler of Egypt, had just committed suicide. It is difficult enough to project ourselves back two thousand years to the world of the Roman Empire, but the first Pharaoh of a united Egypt had donned the Double Crown of Upper and Lower Egypt three thousand years before the birth of Jesus Christ, and the development of the Egyptian culture can be traced back long before that.

The table on page 106 shows in a very simple form an outline of Egyptian chronology. The dates shown are only approximations, but the reader may find the table useful to refer to later on. It may also help the reader to appreciate why the archaeologist in Egypt has such a rich and varied field of subjects to study.

It is the job of the archaeologist to dig for facts, facts that can be sorted, analysed, and turned into history. The task of any archaeologist anywhere is difficult, even if he is investigating a site that no one has disturbed since it was abandoned in antiquity, but people have been investigating the remains of   11

Egyptian civilization for literally thousands of years. Too often, in the words of Sir W. M. Flinders Petrie, one is dealing with "the remains which have escaped the lust of gold, the fury of fanaticism, and the greed of speculators".

The first "tourists" to visit ancient Egyptian monuments were the ancient Egyptians themselves. They scribbled their names, and sometimes pious prayers as well, on the walls. One scribe, for example, who lived during the Eighteenth Dynasty, visited a long-plundered pyramid of the Old Kingdom and compared it with heaven when the sun god was rising there. His comment is still there for all to read, though from the chart it will be seen that even then some 1,200 years separated the scribe from the Pharaoh who built that particular pyramid.

Later still, when Egypt's power had declined so greatly that she was, in the words of the Prophet Isaiah, only a broken reed, the rulers and people alike looked back nostalgically to the glories of the past. They investigated the monuments of their ancestors, revived religious cults, copied inscriptions, and even reproduced whole scenes from old tombs in their own. A priest called Manetho, a contemporary of the first two Ptolemies, wrote a great history of his country, which is now lost, except for a few fragments quoted by other authors whose works have survived.

Introduction
of
Christianity
Curious travellers of the Classical Greek world like Herodotus, the "Father of History", and Diodorus were fascinated by Egypt and wrote accounts of it. The conquering fleet and legions of the Roman Emperor Augustus finally brought Egypt's political independence to a close in 30 B.C., but her culture still survived, and the worship of Isis and Serapis spread throughout the Roman world until in A.D. 384 Christianity gained the upper hand and the Emperor Theodosius ordered the temples of Egypt to be closed.

Egypt remained part of the Christian world of Rome and Byzantium until A.D. 640, when the conquering followers of the Prophet Mohammed swept over her frontiers. By then no one could speak or read the ancient language, and the monuments of the Pharaohs had become objects of mystery and sources of possible wealth. Several fanciful stories have survived of how the pyramids were explored. The Arab writer Masoudi recorded a very colourful account of such an event. According to him, when the pyramid of Cheops was entered

12

The gods Horus and Anubis

during the tenth century, the investigators found chambers whose walls were inlaid with coloured stones and where gold coins were piled up in columns. They also discovered statues, including one of a cock, made of precious stones. When the intrepid explorers entered its chamber, this cock gazed at them with blazing eyes, crowed, and flapped its wings! This and other similarly lively accounts are more reminiscent of the *Arabian Nights* stories than of excavation reports, but they give an idea of the awe which was inspired by the pyramids. No story about them was too fantastic to be believed.

When Europe emerged from the Middle Ages into the modern world Egypt once again began to attract visitors from the West, men like Richard Pococke, who has left us a very entertaining account of the journey he made during the eighteenth century. Such men came, marvelled at all they saw, and collected curios to take home, but none could read the inscriptions that decorated so many ancient buildings.

In 1798 Napoleon Bonaparte, who later became Emperor of France, led an invasion of Egypt. Not the least surprising fact about this whole remarkable venture was that with the army travelled several members of the French Academy, whose formidable task it was to record the inscriptions and to draw the plans of all the monuments they found, besides collecting antiquities to take home. Among the objects that they assembled was a large broken stone, on one side of which was

Early explorers

13

The Rosetta Stone

14

an inscription in three different forms of writing. In 1801 this stone, called the Rosetta Stone after the place where it was found, was given to England with other antiquities as part of the peace settlement of that year. It is now in the British Museum, in London. The Rosetta Stone may not be very exciting to look at, but it was destined to change the whole pattern of studies of ancient Egypt. The event recorded on the Rosetta Stone was written out three times – in Greek, in hieroglyphs, and in Demotic, which is a late, abbreviated form of hieroglyphs. Scholars could already read Greek, so by working with this text, they were able to deduce the meaning of the hieroglyphs as well. The Frenchman Jean François Champollion was the first to publish the answer to the riddle of the ancient script in 1822.

The work of the French academicians and the translation of hieroglyphs gave a great impetus to Europeans' interest in ancient Egypt. It became fashionable to collect Egyptian antiquities, and men made a living by collecting objects in Egypt for sale in Europe. Many ancient tombs were broken into by these collectors, who, unlike the modern archaeologists, were not interested in using the objects to reconstruct the history of Egypt. Their attitude was best summed up by one collector of Mesopotamian antiquities, who said that his aim was to "obtain the largest possible number of well-preserved objects of art at the least possible outlay of time and money". A great deal of priceless information has been lost for ever through their tomb-robbing activities. They were also responsible for a great deal of wanton destruction. Many fragile objects that had survived intact for thousands of years were roughly handled and broken into fragments, although careful archaeological excavation could have preserved them.

One of the most notorious nineteenth-century collectors was an Italian named Giovanni Belzoni, who at one stage in his career had been a strong man in a circus. He was an energetic and ruthless man whose memoirs, though extremely entertaining, show just how much damage he, and people like him, could do. On the hazards of entering an ancient tomb, he records that "a vast quantity of dust rises, so fine that it enters the throat and nostrils, and chokes the nose and mouth. . . ." He goes on to say that one is "surrounded by bodies, by heaps of mummies in all directions . . ." and admits that "it impressed me with horror.... After the exertion of entering such a place ... I sought a resting place, found one and contrived to sit; but when my weight bore on the body of an Egyptian, it crushed like a band box; I naturally had recourse to my hands to sustain my weight, but they found no better support; so that I sank altogether among the broken mummies, with a crash of bones, rags and wooden cases, which raised such a dust as kept me motionless for a quarter of an hour, waiting until it subsided."

Gunpowder Even those whose interest lay in gathering scientific information rather than profitable souvenirs were apt to use methods that make a modern archaeologist's hair stand on end. On his expedition to the Great Pyramid of Gizah, Colonel R. W. Howard-Vyse experienced great difficulties. He found that even the mortar was as hard as stone, and his progress into the pyramid was very slow. Undaunted the Colonel then decided to use gunpowder to blast his way in and notes with simple satisfaction that it was used with great effect.

The scientific approach In the last quarter of the nineteenth century a man whose methods were destined to change the whole approach to archaeology began excavating in Egypt. He was Sir W. M. Flinders Petrie, who was the first to employ scientific methods in excavation. The true value of his system was perhaps best demonstrated at Abydos. In 1899 he took over the concession that had been previously worked by a French expedition under Emile Amélineau. Work was carried out in that area of the necropolis called by the Arabs Um el Qu'ab – the "Mother of Pots" – because of the vast quantity of pottery lying on the surface. Petrie found that the site had been devastated by Amélineau. In his report he wrote bitterly, "Nothing is more disheartening than being obliged to gather results out of the fraction left behind by past plunderers ... the active search in the last four years for everything that could have a value in the eyes of purchasers, or be sold for profit regardless of its source; a search in which whatever was not removed was deliberately and avowedly destroyed in order to enhance the intended profits of European speculators...."

Petrie and his assistants began to clear the site with painstaking precision, recording and measuring every detail. At the end of the work Petrie could announce that he had found the tombs of the first Egyptian Pharaohs. He had traced the development of the architecture of those tombs, he had established the

A Predynastic slate palette in the form of a bird

chronology of the kings of the First Dynasty, and from the smashed fragments of pottery, stone vessels, and ivory furniture, he had revealed the high degree of luxury and sophistication that characterized the life and art of these remarkable people.

During the course of this book we shall be examining the sort of things that can be learned about the ancient Egyptians from excavation. The work of the modern archaeologist is hard, routine detective work. Like a detective, the archaeologist must be able to answer with certainty the questions Who, What, Where, Why, When, and How before he can claim to have solved a problem. In both professions the routine work can sometimes be rather dull, but then suddenly the breakthrough comes. The thrill of that moment of triumph when a new secret of the past is revealed has been vividly described by Howard Carter, who discovered Tutankhamen's tomb: "For a moment, time as a factor in human life has lost its meaning. Three thousand, four thousand years may have gone by, and yet, as you note the signs of recent life around you – the half-filled bowl of mortar before the door, the blackened lamp, the farewell garland dropped upon the threshold, you feel it might

The tomb of Tutankhamen

17

be yesterday. The very air you breathe, unchanged through the centuries, you share with those who laid the mummy to rest."

For the archaeologist it is the uncertain nature of his business that makes it so exciting. The unexpected can happen at any time. To give just one example of this, in the 1894 edition of his *History of Egypt*, Petrie wrote that the history of the early dynasties was a blank, yet within a few years Petrie himself had filled that blank. He and his associates excavated cemeteries not only of the first three dynasties, but also of the people of the Predynastic Period, as well. Within ten years he had revealed evidence of a thousand years of history.

Objects that are valueless in themselves are often of the utmost historical importance. One day in 1887 a woman looking for fertilizer in the ruins of Tell el Amarna found a store of broken clay tablets. She put them in a sack and took them to a dealer. They looked very unpromising material, but they turned out to be letters from foreign kings to the Egyptian Pharaoh. The woman had discovered the "Foreign Office" of the Pharaoh Akhenaten!

A few rather poor beads and bits of pottery may be of more use in dating a culture than beautiful objects of precious metal, but archaeologists are only human, after all, and somehow there is a special thrill in finding gold. Archaeology has long ceased to be a treasure hunt, but it cannot be denied that a rich find does capture the imagination of scholar and layman alike. Therefore it is perhaps only right to leave the last word on this subject to Howard Carter, the discoverer of the greatest treasure of all. On the opening of the tomb of Tutankhamen, he records: "At first I could see nothing, the hot air escaping from the tomb causing the candle flame to flicker. But presently, as my eyes grew accustomed to the light, details of the room emerged slowly from the mist; strange animals, statues, and gold – everywhere the glint of gold. For a moment – an eternity it must have seemed to the others standing by – I was struck dumb; then Lord Carnarvon inquired anxiously – "Can you see anything?"

"'Yes,' I replied, '. . . wonderful things. . . .'"

CHAPTER TWO

Egypt – The Land, and the Life and Problems of the Archaeologists Who Work There

A WORD OF WARNING

In some countries, particularly where the excavation seasons are short, volunteer helpers are welcomed by archaeologists. In Great Britain, for example, there are usually excavations in progress during Easter and summer vacations, where students can spend holiday time as volunteer helpers. In the United States, however, the student must be usually studying archaeology before being invited to work on an excavation.

Amateurs and professionals

ORGANIZING AN EXPEDITION

The number of excavations conducted by foreign archaeologists in Egypt at any one time is limited by the high cost of mounting such an expedition. Expeditions are organized by a museum, a university, or a learned society, and they have to be able to meet the cost themselves, though they can probably obtain some help from government grants and private subscriptions as well, if they are lucky. The days when an interested millionaire hired an archaeologist and mounted a whole excavation from his own purse seem to have gone for ever.

Permission to dig at any site has to be obtained from the government of the United Arab Republic. Once such a concession has been granted, the committee organizing the expedition and its chosen field director must get their excavation team together. As Cairo is some 2,000 miles from London and more than twice that distance from New York, and as an excavation season in Egypt can last for five months, it is clearly impossible for the field director to use volunteer amateur helpers, however enthusiastic they may be.

In these circumstances, who does go on an archaeological expedition to Egypt? The team is usually made up of students who are studying Egyptology at a college or university, professional archaeologists, and others who are recognized experts

19

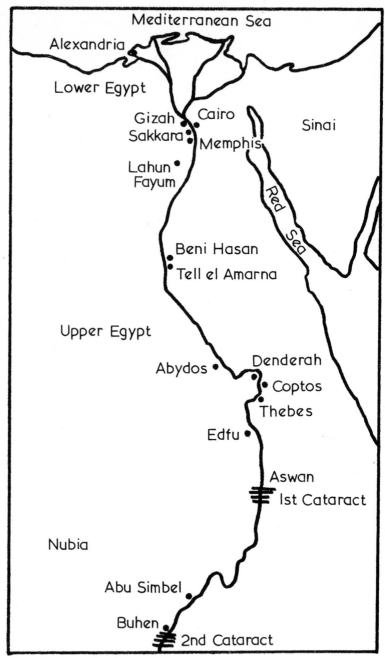

A sketch map of Egypt

Mediterranean Sea

Alexandria

Lower Egypt

Gizah   Cairo
Sakkara   Memphis   Sinai

Lahun
Fayum

Red Sea

Beni Hasan
Tell el Amarna

Upper Egypt

Abydos   Denderah
Coptos
Thebes
Edfu

Aswan
1st Cataract

Nubia

Abu Simbel

Buhen
2nd Cataract

20

in their own fields. To give a few examples, most expeditions usually require the services of an architect and surveyor. There is always need for a good photographer, and a linguist is essential if inscriptions are likely to be found. If the excavation is within easy reach of Cairo the assistance of the technicians of the Department of Antiquities there may be obtained. If, on the other hand, the concession is in a remote area a conservationist, who can treat fragile objects as they come out of the ground, is a useful person to have on the staff. Obviously, the more money an expedition has, the more experts it can afford to take.

THE LAND AND THE RIVER

Herodotus referred to Egypt as the gift of the Nile. The ancient Egyptians themselves were very conscious of the debt they owed to the river, and they worshipped it as a god, whom they called Hapy.

> "Praise to you, O Nile! Greetings, O Nile!
> For you come from afar
> To keep Egypt alive!"

The Nile

The Nile is one of the world's longest rivers. Rising in the area of the lakes of Central Africa, the White Nile begins the first stage of its 4,000-mile journey northward to the sea through the varied scenery of Uganda and the Southern Sudan. Along the way it is fed by several minor tributaries, but when it reaches Khartoum, it is joined by the Blue Nile and from then on is "the Nile". Only one tributary enters the Nile north of Khartoum – the Atbara. The Blue Nile rises in Lake Tana in the Abyssinian Highlands, and the heavy rains in this area, lasting from June to September, send torrents of water raging down the Blue Nile and the Atbara into the Nile proper. Before the building of modern dams, this used to result in the annual flooding, or Inundation, of Egypt.

When the Nile flows north from Khartoum it is destined by a curious freak of nature to run through desert. In the places where the river has carved itself a broad valley to run through the banks are fertile for several miles, but in others the desert cliffs rise sharply from the water's edge, and in places the rocks cross the course of the river, forming the barriers of the Six Cataracts. In Upper Egypt one can always see the desert cliffs.

Sometimes they tower close at hand, while at others they stand like a defensive wall on the horizon, but one is always conscious of them. From Khartoum northward the Nubian cliffs are sandstone, but at Aswan it is a granite outcrop spilling into the river that causes the First Cataract. The sandstone then reappears until, in the area of Esnah, it gives way to limestone, which stretches to Cairo.

At Cairo the cliffs end, and the river divides and flows on to the Mediterranean, the "Great Green", as the Egyptians called it, through several different channels. This is the area of the Delta, or Lower Egypt, low-lying and fertile, built up by centuries of mud washed down by the Inundation.

Rain is almost unknown in Egypt. Cairo gets up to 6 cm of rain a year, and Alexandria may get 24 cm, most of it in January. For water, therefore, Egypt was always dependent on the river. In order to make the best use of the available water the Egyptians, from the very earliest times, developed a complex system of irrigation canals to carry water to outlying fields. The land that was reached by the water and silt of the Inundation was rich and fertile, supporting two crops a year in some places, but, where the waters did not reach, there was desert. It is still possible to stand with one foot in a green field and the other in desert sand.

Inundations and famines In the years of good Inundations there was abundance; in a bad year there was famine. "Behold, there come seven years of great plenty throughout all the land of Egypt: And there shall arise after them seven years of famine; and all the plenty shall be forgotten in the land of Egypt; and the famine shall consume the land" (Genesis 41:29–30). The background of the story of Joseph and Pharaoh's dream was all too familiar to the inhabitants of Pharaonic Egypt; in fact, the Egyptians themselves had their own story of a famous famine. The Famine Stela, carved on a rock on the island of Sehel, just south of Elephantine, tells how, in the reign of King Zoser, Egypt suffered from famine, with seven years of poor Inundations. Zoser appealed to his adviser, Imhotep, for advice, and was told that Khnum, the ram-headed lord of the Cataract, was angry. Zoser immediately made Khnum a large grant of land where a magnificent temple could be built, and the grateful deity then sent good Inundations, and so the famine ended.

22   You cannot visit Egypt without being acutely aware of the

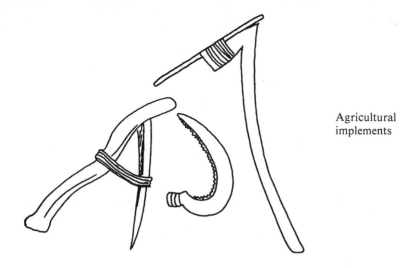

contrasting nature of the countryside and of the importance of
the river. In the valley you may not be able to see the river itself
all the time, for it may be several miles away, hidden behind
palm trees, but you cannot walk many yards off a road without
seeing the network of irrigation canals and ditches which are
supplied by the river. If you stand quietly and listen you can
usually hear the rhythmic creak of *sakiyah* (a water wheel
worked by an animal), of *shaduf*, and of Archimedes' screw,
raising and transferring water from one place to another. This
is the cultivated land, the "Black Land", as ancient Egyptians
called it because of the rich black mud. The valley is a flat
patchwork of vivid green fields and shady palm groves, which
shelter villages from the blazing sun. The roads are straight,
following the lines of the irrigation canals, and lined with trees.
Above all is the vast arc of the sky, almost invariably blue,
which provides a back-cloth of dazzling beauty for the flocks of
white egrets that rise suddenly from the cultivation, and for the
hawks that wheel and glide high above, watching all that goes
on. To the ancient Egyptians the hawk was the symbol of
Horus, god of the sky, whose two blazing eyes were the sun and
the moon. Sounds carry far in the clear air, and among them is
always the unmelodious bray of a donkey, bitterly lamenting
his lowly station in life. On either side rise the desert cliffs, the
"Red Land", which was the domain of the wicked god Set
and the fierce lioness goddess Sekhmet. Some people feel

*The
"Black Land"*

23

unpleasantly boxed in by the cliffs, but they gave the ancient Egyptians a sense of security, a feeling that there was a rampart of rock protecting them from their enemies outside. This was reflected in their speech, and to call a man "highlander" or "dweller in the uplands" was to call him a foreigner and outsider.

The *"Red Land"* Once you are standing on the top of the cliffs, the desert stretches away before you. The air is very clear, and you can see for miles. The desert has a beauty all of its own, changing colour during the day as the sun varies in height. The rocks and sand are dull, uninteresting yellows and browns in early morning, but as the sun strikes them they turn pink and pale yellow, then become almost white in the heat of the day, and finally turn a beautiful gold in the late afternoon, until the sun slips over the horizon in a blaze of crimson glory. At night, unhindered by clouds or a smoke-polluted atmosphere, the sky is radiant, with more stars than one ever sees in the industrial cities of the north. No wonder the ancients made such a study of the stars!

By now the reader may be wondering what all this geographical information has to do with archaeology. The answer is, a very great deal. Until you know what a country's physical characteristics are, you cannot appreciate the problems that beset an archaeologist's investigations.

THE PROBLEMS

All archaeologists, no matter where they excavate, have their own special problems, and Egyptologists are no exception, though with such a glorious climate, friendly people, and accessible sites, some might consider them far better off than most! In Egypt some of the difficulties which the archaeologist encounters are peculiar to one area; others are present in the whole country. Let us examine a few of both kinds.

Sand It has been pointed out that every foot of land watered by the Inundation was very valuable. The residents of Upper Egypt, therefore, always buried their dead in the desert so as not to waste land that could be cultivated. For religious reasons they usually chose the Western Desert, because it was here that the sun god "died" every evening and descended into the Underworld. Thanks to the warm, dry sand in which they were buried, many objects and bodies have been found in an extra-

24

North Sakkara with a view of the pyramids of Abusir and Gizah in the distance

ordinarily good state of preservation. This same climate, *Termites* however, also suits the termite, or "white ant", very well. An archaeologist may enter a tomb that has escaped the attentions of tomb robbers, only to find that the white ant has worked a havoc of destruction among all the grave goods made of wood.

One of the greatest obstacles that can hinder an archaeologist in Upper Egypt is sand – tons and tons of it – that must be sifted and shifted before one reaches what one is looking for. This is not the place to discuss the relative advantages of various excavating techniques, but it must be pointed out that, whereas in firm soil a system of cutting trenches can be employed, you just cannot dig neat, straight-sided trenches in sand, as the sides will collapse. In loose sand you have to clear a large area by removing hundreds of tons of sand, layer by layer.

Now, it is all very easy to say "clear a large area", but where do you put all the sand? The answer is that you make a large 25 dump, but archaeologists' dumps can be exasperating obstacles in themselves. Just imagine for a moment how you would feel if you unexpectedly came across an important-looking wall and started digging it out, only to find that it was heading straight for a huge mound of rubble that someone had dumped fifty years earlier. It is even worse if, by a horrid mischance, it is a dump you made yourself the previous season because your trial trenches had failed to reveal anything in that area! A great deal of money that one can ill afford may have to be spent on shifting the mountains of debris.

Whereas in Upper Egypt sand can be a big problem, in Lower Egypt water is more likely to present the greatest difficulty. The Delta, it must be remembered, is low-lying ground built up by the silt deposited by the Inundation. When one starts to dig down in the Delta, water soon begins to seep into the trenches, and pumps may be necessary to drain them. As the Egyptians used sun-dried mud bricks to build their houses, there will be few traces of them left in soil which has been annually flooded for centuries.

Town sites   Villages had to be built on any available high ground so as to avoid the waters of the Inundation. Rather than put valuable land out of cultivation, the same sites were used over and over again for houses, and many sites are still being used today. Thus, numerous ancient town sites are not available for excavation because a modern town or village has been built directly above them. The village, fields, and palm groves of modern Mitrahinah, for example, are over the site of Memphis, the capital of Egypt during the Old Kingdom, and modern Luxor is built on the ruins of Thebes, capital of Egypt during the New Kingdom, when Egypt ruled the Near East.

Many of the "tells" in the Delta, the great mounds that are the remains of ancient cities, are free of modern buildings, but anyone who has seen the gigantic size of a place like Tanis will appreciate that to excavate such a site thoroughly would require vast sums of money not readily available in these days of high taxes and government squeezes.

Unfortunately for the archaeologist, it was found that ancient mud bricks break down into a useful fertilizer known as *sabakh*. Many an expedition has found that, instead of a nice stratified site, with the most recent things on top and the most ancient things at the bottom of the mound, they are dealing

26

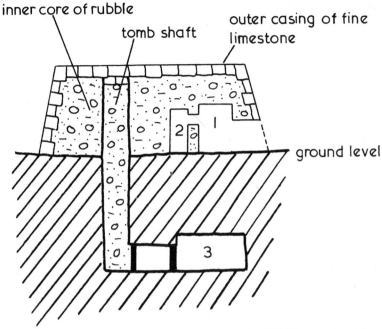

inner core of rubble

tomb shaft

outer casing of fine limestone

ground level

An Old Kingdom mastaba

I Chapel

2 Serdab (statue chamber)

3 Burial chamber

with a site that has been turned topsy turvy by generations of *fellahin* (Egyptian peasants) in search of fertilizer!

"... but it had been robbed in antiquity." How often one comes across these words in an excavation report! During the three thousand years of the recorded history of Pharaonic Egypt, a criminal element in society made a habit of robbing the graves of the sacred dead. Some robberies did not occur for centuries after the original burial, but some took place within a very short space of time. In a cemetery of the courtiers who were buried near a pyramid of their Pharaoh during the Middle Kingdom, the excavators on an expedition run by the Metropolitan Museum of Art of New York discovered robbers' galleries cut through tombs *directly* to the burial chamber—evidence that the robbers must have been led by a dishonest

Tomb robbers

27

Ramesses II

priest or workman who knew exactly where the most valuable goods were located.

In times of national disturbance an effective watch could not be kept, even over the royal tombs. During the Twentieth and Twenty-first dynasties things were so bad that the priests were obliged to gather the remaining royal mummies together and bury them secretly, away from their original tombs. Consider the size of the treasure buried with Tutankhamen. He was a minor king who reigned only nine years, and he was buried in a small four-roomed tomb. Compare the size of his tomb with the enormous ones of important Pharaohs like Tuthmosis III, Seti I, and Ramesses II, and think of the wealth that must have been buried with *them*! Then one really cannot be surprised that the temptation proved too much for many. When the New Kingdom was at the peak of its greatness, the Valley of the Kings was a storehouse for more wealth, both in pure bullion and in artistic craftsmanship, than any other place on earth.

A papyrus has survived which records the interrogation of a group of men who had robbed the Royal Necropolis. One man describes how he and his companions broke into one tomb, where they found a king and his queen buried together, surrounded by treasure of gold, silver, and bronze. The man refers to the deceased king as a god, but this did not prevent him and his confederates from breaking open the golden coffins and stripping off the gold and jewels which decked the royal mummies.

During the Middle Ages in Europe, mummies from Egypt were in demand for medicines, so tombs were robbed to supply the demand, and yet more archaeological material was destroyed.

In the early nineteenth century, before the need for scientific investigation was recognized, some European collectors were buying all the curios of the ancient world that they could find, and tomb robbing once again came into vogue, especially among the villagers of Gurneh, which is situated among the tombs of the nobles of Thebes. In some cases it was these very robbers who led archaeologists to great discoveries. It was a Gurneh villager who first discovered the hidden cache of royal mummies mentioned above, and people from the same village were also the first to discover the tomb of three of the ladies of the harem of Tuthmosis III. When the mummies of the

The villagers of Gurneh

29

Pharaohs were loaded on to a steamer to be taken to Cairo it is said that a crowd of peasant women ran along the bank, shrieking and tearing their hair, just as once their ancestors had mourned these very kings when they had been laid to rest in their tombs.

One other difficulty that faces the Egyptologist is that the Egyptians, Pharaohs, nobles, and commoners alike, quite happily took over and reused many of their ancestors' buildings and tombs. Ramesses the Great, for example, blocked out the names of his predecessors and substituted his own on buildings all over Egypt, while tombs have been found which were robbed and reused several times. The Pharaohs were perfectly capable of using one another's buildings as stone quarries. For example, one of the great pylons at Karnak has yielded thousands of fragments of a building of Akhenaten which had been demolished and the stones smashed and used as fill.

LIFE ON AN EXCAVATION

When I was first invited to join an expedition, I was absolutely delighted, of course, but I had just finished reading the adventures of the eighteenth-century traveller Pococke, and I must admit that I had a few misgivings. Vague pictures flitted across my mind of myself lying in a tent infested with snakes and scorpions and with jackals howling outside. Let me hasten to reassure any would-be archaeologist that *nothing* could be farther from the truth. You may just possibly have to live in a tent if you join an expedition that is going to an inaccessible area *Home comforts* where there has been no previous excavation, but most of the major archaeological sites have already been partially excavated, and perfectly good houses have been erected there. If a house is not available and an expedition plans to work in the area for some time, it will build itself a house near the concession. As for snakes, scorpions, and jackals, the only place you are likely to see them is in the spacious gardens of the Cairo Zoo.

An excavation season in Upper Egypt can take place any time between November and April, but beyond this period the heat can make working conditions uncomfortable. In the Delta, however, work may not begin till the spring, for by then the soil will have had time to dry out. Excavation will cease with 30 the coming of the worst of the summer heat.

If the field director is a married man he will probably take his wife with him to supervise the domestic arrangements. As the excavation staff will be fully occupied with the dig all day, there will have to be some Egyptian *suffragis* on the staff to keep the house clean and cook the meals. At the end of a hard day, when you are walking back across the sand, aching in muscles that you did not know you possessed, it is very comforting to see the flutter of a white tunic in the distance and to know that one of the *suffragis* is waiting to welcome you back with a friendly grin, some hot water for a much-needed wash, and the reassurance that there is a good dinner being prepared. If the dinner happens to be pigeons, then you are in for an extra treat. One of the most glorious smells I know is that of pigeons being grilled over a charcoal fire in the clear, sweet air of an Egyptian night.

One important member of any expedition is the Egyptian inspector. Egypt is divided up into several districts by the Department of Antiquities, and over each one is a chief inspector and his staff, whose task it is to care for the monuments in their area and to excavate new ones. An inspector is also attached to every foreign expedition to help and advise.

Dig houses and bungalows may vary in size, but they usually have a large room which acts as a dining room and lounge, where members of the expedition eat together and then gather and talk. The discussions are usually "shop" in one form or another: the digs and personalities of the past, the progress of the present expedition, and plans for the future. There is usually a small bedroom for each member of the staff, and a fully equipped bathroom. An important part of any dig house is the magazine, where the antiquities are stored and where one does all the necessary work on them. Here also maps and plans are drawn, and the pottery catalogue will be found spreading across the walls as more and more types of pottery are identified and drawn.

I was very lucky, because the dig house I stayed in at Sakkara had a garden. Though this bungalow is perched up on the ridge of the Western Desert, a charming little garden has been won from the sand by years of patient labour, and it provides a beautiful green haven of rest for leisure moments. It is a very peaceful place to sit and listen to the song of the sparrows that always gather around the house. Here the sounds 31 from the valley only occasionally intrude, such as when one of the numerous dogs decides to give voice and sets off the other dogs in the neighbourhood. Any dig house is likely to attract some dogs. These animals do not belong to anyone but live by scavenging in their own well-defined territories. Though half wild, they soon become very affectionate if you feed them, greeting your return at the end of the day with a positive frenzy of enthusiasm. Once a certain number of dogs have adopted you, they will allow no animal from another pack to intrude. If any new dog puts one paw over the invisible line that marks a territorial boundary he is driven off at great speed. Though their nocturnal serenades to the full moon can be rather trying, they are otherwise very useful as watch dogs. You always know when a stranger is approaching, because the whole pack of dogs will stream out in full cry.

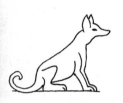

An Ancient
Egyptian pet dog

If you are on an expedition that is camped in the desert a long way from the nearest village, you may find that your water has to be brought up to you on camel back. If this is the case, be careful. Though docile enough with their owners, these grumpy animals respect no one's dignity but their own, and they have a mouthful of very large teeth.

In Egypt the sites are often very large and enormous quantities of sand have to be moved, so it is customary to hire a force of local labour to do the actual digging. The numbers recruited can vary between a dozen and three hundred or so, depending on the nature of the site and the amount of money available. The workmen are under the control of a *reis*, or foreman, who keeps the work running smoothly. Next to him in

Guftis

importance are the *Guftis*. These men are so called because Guft is their home town. During the last years of the last century, Sir Flinders Petrie gathered together a force of *Guftis* whom he trained in the techniques of excavation. He took them with him on all his digs, and they became the acknowledged experts in their craft. They passed their skills on to their sons, and now if any expedition needs expert workmen, it sends for *Guftis*, who arrive with all their luggage and camp on the site for the season.

The *Guftis* are far outnumbered by the workmen who are recruited from the villages around the site. The whole working body is divided between *tourieh* men and basket boys. The

32   *tourieh* is a digging instrument with which the sand is scraped

Excavation work in progress

into a basket. It needs several basket boys to keep one *tourieh* man busy. The basket boys then jog along in long, winding lines, carrying the sand to the dumps.

No force of workmen is complete without its singer. This gentleman has a fine repertoire of songs, both traditional and improvised, which he sings for hours at a time at the top of his voice to encourage the men and to keep them moving in a steady rhythm. He is particularly useful if there is a heavy object to be shifted. Having seen a really enormous block of stone being hauled along in time with a special chant gives one some idea how the ancient Egyptians managed to build the pyramids without any mechanical aids. Your first impression of a dig is likely to be of a vast cloud of dust flying in the distance, from which rises the voice of a singer who, as you appear, breaks into a song of welcome in which the men join.

The hours of work on a dig can vary with the personal preference of the *mudir*, the field director, but it is common practice for the work to begin early, perhaps at 6 a.m. This may be unpleasantly early, but it has its compensations. Early on a winter's morning at Sakkara, for example, there is usually a lot of mist about. It rises from the river, obscuring the valley completely, and swirls up over the edge of the hill and across the desert. As the sun rises over the cliffs of the Eastern Desert, it lights all the high landmarks of the area. Suddenly the top of the Step Pyramid of Zoser swims up out of the mist, bathed in the pale morning sunshine. Then, to the north, the pyramids of Abusir and Gizah, tiny at this distance, appear to float on a sea of mist. As the sun rises higher, the tops of the palm trees show in the valley; the mist then rapidly thins, and the whole valley is clear by nine o'clock.

If work begins at 6 a.m., there will be a pause for breakfast and a rest at about 9 a.m., and the work will finish about 2 p.m. The members of the expedition staff work on the dig in shifts if things are quiet, but they may all be needed if many important objects start coming up in rapid succession. When you are on duty on the dig, your job is one of general supervision. Objects must be recorded as they are found, photographed in position, and their exact location noted so that they can later be added to the master plan of the building or area being studied. Only when all possible information has been gathered on the spot can the objects be removed and sent to the workroom, where a detailed examination can be made.

The recording
of finds   When an object arrives in the workroom, it usually needs to be cleaned, and it may need some emergency repairs. Each object has to be drawn, and all details of material, style, where it was found, its date if known, and so on must be put with the drawing. The object is then labelled, photographed, and recorded in a register, which will go to the Egyptian Antiquities Service, where a record is kept of all objects found in Egypt. If the object has an inscription, it must be copied and translated. When a pot is discovered, it must be compared with the pottery already excavated. If a similar vessel has been found previously, then it can be given the same type number, but if it is a new type, a drawing of it must be added to the illustrated list of pottery finds. If buildings are being excavated, these have to be measured and drawn and a reconstruction made if possible, and then they have to be plotted on the map of the
34   concession, which will have been made when the site was first

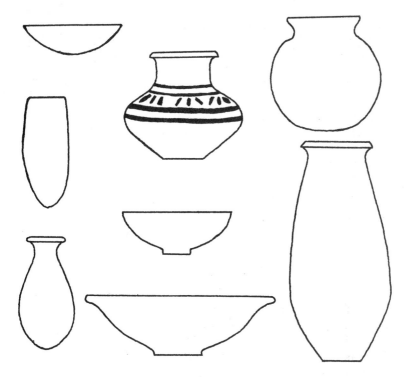

Egyptian pottery of the Eighteenth Dynasty

surveyed. Finally, the field director keeps a day-by-day diary in which all the work and finds are recorded.

This may seem like an awful lot of wasted time and energy, but it must be remembered that when the excavator has returned home, maybe to London, Paris, or New York, he may wish to write an article about an object which is in Cairo, so he will need every fact about it to be clearly set out for him to refer to. Moreover, a site may take several years to excavate completely, and it may be some time after that before the field director can publish his findings as a whole. In these circumstances it is useless to rely on one's memory for details. Every fact and measurement must be recorded at the time, or it will be lost for ever. An object may be very beautiful in itself, but unless all the fact about it are known, it is of little value to the historian.

If the excavation is quiet, the job of recording the finds can be done during the hours of digging, leaving you a fair amount of free time later in which to do your own work or to visit monuments of interest in the area. Such times of comparative tranquillity may not last long. Suddenly, often when you are least expecting it, a shout goes up from one corner of the site, and everyone rushes to where a delighted workman is waving in triumph. If a really big discovery has been made, you are likely to be up all night, drawing and recording till your fingers are numb and you begin to wonder why on earth you ever wanted to be an archaeologist in the first place! But it is all worth it. Nothing can equal the thrill of anticipation as you see something emerging from the sand that has been lost to the world for two, three, four, or five thousand years. Nothing can surpass the quiet satisfaction that you feel as, thanks to your efforts, the desert gives up a secret and one more piece of the jigsaw puzzle of the past slips quietly into place.

Cartouche of Tutankhamen

Because of the wealth of the burial of Tutankhamen and the worldwide interest that its discovery aroused, archaeology, and Egyptian archaeology in particular, is considered "news". If an excavation uncovers something interesting on one day, the next morning the field director may find himself surrounded by reporters and wishing that he had brought a public relations officer along with the expedition! The trouble is that treasure is news, but an uninteresting-looking object, even if it answers a problem that has been puzzling scholars for years, will not be exciting enough for many of the general public.

"Pharaoh's Curse"

Since the subject of Tutankhamen has been raised, it might be as well to mention the "Pharaoh's Curse". I am sorry to disappoint the romantically minded, but the story is a myth, and there is *no* curse written above the doorway of his tomb. The nearest thing known to a curse comes from the tombs of certain Old Kingdom noblemen who lived a thousand years before Tutankhamen. They usually say something like this: "As to anything which you may do against this my tomb of the Necropolis, the same shall be done against your property." Or, "Any noble, any official, or any man who may destroy any stone or any brick in this my tomb will be judged by the Great God." The threats are definitely there, but they have nothing to do with Pharaohs in general or Tutankhamen in particular. It is true that Lord Carnarvon died within a few months of the opening of the tomb and that two other Egyptologists also died

36

shortly afterwards, but these are just unhappy coincidences. If one examines the list of those who were among the first to enter the tomb, it will be seen that they lived, or are living, a normal life span.

Toward the end of a successful season the excavation staff has to face the prospect of a division. Objects found in Egypt obviously belong to the Egyptian people, and it is only right that unique pieces should remain in Egypt; but it is also reasonable that the expeditions should be rewarded for all their efforts and expenses by giving them a share in the objects found. A site can produce many objects of the same type; for example, there may be dozens of bronze votive figures of one particular deity. In this case the Egyptian Government, through the agency of the Antiquities Service, will retain a few examples, giving the rest to the expedition. After the division comes the nerve-racking business of packing the objects for transportation home. When an object has survived intact for several thousand years, it would be a tragedy if, thanks to one's inadequate packing, it should be broken on the way home!

CHAPTER THREE

Daily Life in Ancient Egypt as Revealed by Tombs, Towns, Tomb Paintings, and Inscriptions

The importance of writing

The archaeologist is concerned with finding out about the life of ancient man by investigating and analysing his material remains. Man has been living on earth for about two million years, and during that time has left plenty of remains behind for archaeologists to study, but it was only five thousand or so years ago that man learned to write, and so acquired a skill which enabled him to share his thoughts with future generations. Palaeolithic hunters and neolithic farmers in many parts of the world had no system of writing at all, while some more advanced civilizations have left behind inscriptions which have as yet defied all attempts to interpret them. Cretan Linear A and Etruscan are two such scripts. Archaeologists in these fields are therefore at a disadvantage compared with the Egyptologist, because in Egypt the evidence of material objects is supplemented by numerous documents which can be translated, thanks to the work of Champollion and his successors. In this chapter we are going to examine what archaeologists have found out about the life of Egyptians of the Pharaonic period from the objects that have survived, and this will be supplemented by the knowledge gained from the documents.

Egyptologists are particularly fortunate because, besides material remains and documentary sources, they have a unique record of daily life in ancient Egypt in the form of tomb paintings and reliefs. The pictures that cover the walls of so many tombs were not simply decorative or commemorative in character; they also had a strictly practical aspect. The scenes on tomb walls were invested with magical properties. It was believed that if the dead man was shown before a table loaded with food and the proper formula was inscribed by it, then, by magic, this food would be always available to him in the Hereafter. It has often been suggested that the ancient Egyptians were a morbid race, obsessed with death. In fact, they loved life so

38

much that they hoped the Next World would be a perfected version of it. The Egyptian nobleman therefore decorated his tomb with scenes from his daily life which he hoped would be magically repeated throughout eternity. He also stored in his tomb all the things he would need in the Next World, so the Egyptologist has a series of scenes of daily life set out for him in many tombs, besides many of the actual objects in daily use.

HOUSING

It was stated in Chapter Two that little excavation has been done in Egyptian town sites because there are comparatively few available. There are some notable exceptions, however, as some examples of domestic architecture have been available for study.

Tell el Amarna was the capital city of the heretic Pharaoh *A villa* Akhenaten, who reigned from about 1379 to 1362 B.C. It was *at Amarna* built and abandoned within twenty years and was not built over again until a comparatively recent date, when two villages grew up and began to encroach on part of the site. At Tell el Amarna, therefore, archaeologists have had a chance to excavate the dwellings of citizens of all classes. The excavators found that the noblemen at Amarna lived in large pleasant villas situated in spacious grounds, around which high walls were built to protect them from the curious eyes of passers-by in the street. Grouped around the main houses were the nobleman's gardens, stables, well, grain bins, storehouses, servants' quarters, and kitchens, the latter being placed away from the main house to keep unpleasant odours from offending the sensitive nostrils of the master and his family.

The typical villa was usually square in shape, with the central hall taller than the rest of the building so that light could enter from windows set at ceiling level. In a land of heat and bright sunlight such as Egypt, small windows are quite adequate, anyway.

The house was only one storey high, but there were stairs to give access to the flat roof, where the family might spend a good deal of time. In several houses the excavators found extra column bases which did not belong to the ground-floor rooms, showing that there had been some light structure on the roof. These structures, or "kiosks", usually had three walls and a roof, the fourth side being open except for the columns

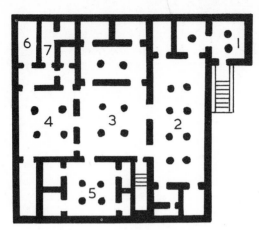

1 Porch
2 West loggia
3 Central hall
4 Inner reception roo[m]
5 North loggia
6 Master bedroom
7 Bathroom

An Amarna villa

supporting the roof, and were situated on the north side of the house so they were a protection from the worst of the sun and also got the most benefit from the cool breeze which blew from the north.

The ancient Egyptian noblemen paid great attention to personal hygiene, and their houses were equipped with bathrooms and toilets.

All houses, and indeed palaces, too, were built of mud brick. Stone was for temples and tombs, which had to last for all eternity. The columns and roofing beams of a house were made of wood, and, when the owner could afford it, stone was used for column bases and door steps. Excavations revealed that the walls of the rooms were covered with a fine plaster and then painted in bright colours. Some of the decorations were formal flower motifs, but others were delightfully naturalistic in design. At the Palace of Malkata, for example, one room was decorated with pictures of calves gambolling among papyrus reeds.

The less affluent citizens of Amarna had to be content with smaller houses and fewer amenities. Their houses had several rooms, but they lacked the gardens which the noblemen delighted in.

To the east of the city, near the desert edge, was a separate village which housed the men who were working on the tombs in the cliffs. The village was built on a square plan and was surrounded by walls, broken only by one gate on the southern side. Just inside this gate was an open area or public place,

40

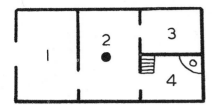

1 Entrance hall

2 Living room

3 Bedroom

4 Kitchen with stairs to roof

which seems to have had a shrine built against the south wall. The foreman's house, which was larger than all the rest, was built in the southeast corner of the square. Apart from this, there was a depressing note of regimentation about the rest of the village. There were five straight streets separating six rows of small houses, all running north–south. All the little houses measured approximately five by ten metres, and each had four rooms. Each had one door, leading directly from the street into an entrance hall. Here the owner might work at his craft and stable a donkey or cow if he owned one. From the entrance hall one passed into the main living room, the roof of which was supported by a single column. Behind the living room were a small bedroom, a kitchen with a hole in the roof to let out the smoke, and stairs leading to the roof. The walls of the houses were too thin to support a second storey, but, as with the noblemen's houses, there was usually some light structure on the roof. It seems that the women and children spent a lot of their time up there, for on top of the debris of the fallen roofs, spindles, pots, and toys were found, showing that these had been on the roof when it collapsed.

Because Akhenaten moved his capital to a virgin site, his town planners could provide pleasant villas set in spacious gardens for those who could afford them. But in ancient cities like Thebes and Memphis, where land was scarce, houses were packed closely together. These cities are not available for excavation, but the stylized pictures of houses that the Egyptians themselves painted, together with a few pottery

41

models that they made of them, enable us to make certain deductions. Town houses seem to have been tall, narrow build-

A town house ings of two, three, and even four storeys. Servants and crafts-men attached to the owner of the house worked in the ground-floor rooms; the stores were also kept on the ground floor, or perhaps in some cases in cellars. The master and his family, therefore, occupied the upper rooms. All houses had the usual flat roof, where on hot summer evenings the family would sit to catch the refreshing cool breeze coming up from the river.

There is no evidence available to show what the houses of the peasants were like, but most probably they were like the dwellings of all peasants down through the ages – small one- or two-roomed affairs where men and their animals sheltered together.

BUILDING TECHNIQUES

Mud bricks It has been pointed out that all domestic buildings were made of mud bricks. These bricks were made by mixing Nile mud and water with straw or sand, which acted as a very necessary binding agent. It will be remembered that during their sojourn in Egypt the Children of Israel ran into difficulties on this point. "And Pharaoh commanded the same day the taskmasters of the people, and their officers, saying, Ye shall no more give the people straw to make brick, as heretofore: let them go and gather straw for themselves" (Exodus 5:6–7). The mixture of mud and straw was put into wooden moulds and left to dry in the hot sun. A building of this sun-dried brick is a perfectly prac-tical proposition in a country such as Egypt where there is little or no rainfall. The tomb of Rekhmire at Thebes has scenes showing how bricks were made. One can feel very sorry for the men mixing the mud by endlessly treading it with their feet under the blazing sun and the watchful eye of the overseer.

One-storeyed houses built of mud brick, which does not need to be cemented into place, are comparatively easy to construct in a short space of time. The visitor who wanders around the ruins of the city of Akhenaten at Tell el Amarna or the palace of Amenhotep III at Malkata may be impressed by the size of what he sees, but not by the individual buildings. His real admiration is rightly reserved for the pyramids, tombs, and temples built of stone. When gazing at the Great Pyramid of

42 Cheops at Gizah, it is difficult to remember that this and all the

other gigantic monuments were built without mechanical aids. The first thing that strikes the visitor to Gizah, for example, is simply the incredible size. One can read in cold print that the base of Cheops' Pyramid is some 230 metres square, that some 2,300,000 blocks, each averaging close to three *tonnes* in weight, were used in its construction, and that the area of its base could accommodate five of Europe's greatest cathedrals, and may still be unprepared for the effects of that majestic bulk rising into the sky. Then, and only then, one comes to a realization of the achievements and abilities of ancient peoples.

The main types of stone used for building were limestone, sandstone, and granite. There were several limestone quarries in Egypt, but the highest-quality stone came from the quarries at Tura, just south of Cairo. The principal sandstone quarries were at Gebel el Silsileh, and granite came from Aswan. The tools used in quarrying were metal chisels (which were of copper until the Middle Kingdom, when bronze became common), wooden mallets, stone hammers, and wooden wedges, which were pounded in to split blocks of stone from the sides of the quarry. The marks of these tools are still visible in some ancient quarries, together with the tools themselves and blocks of stone that for some reason were never used. *Building in stone*

When a block of stone had been quarried, it had to be hauled to the river, floated on a barge to its destination, and then hauled again, often a considerable distance, to the building site. All this was accomplished by using only ropes, sledges, rollers, and many, many pairs of strong arms.

When a new temple or tomb was required, the architect drew up his plans on a papyrus roll. One such plan, that of the tomb of Ramesses IV, has survived and is now in the Turin Museum. After the site had been chosen and levelled, a great foundation ceremony was held, during which foundation deposits were placed in special pits. These deposits consisted of such things as plaques and bricks, some made of precious stones and metals, bearing the name of the Pharaoh, and model tools were also included. If the building was to be a really important one, such as the Pharaoh's mortuary temple, the whole court would be present at the foundation ceremonies, which would then be shown on the temple wall, presided over by the goddess Seshat, who was the patroness of letters and calculation.

The ceremonies over, the temple would be marked out 43

according to the architect's plan, the foundations laid, and the first course of stone dragged into place. When a building was being erected, huge ramps of sand and rubble were also constructed. These were enlarged as the building grew in height so that the stones could be dragged up to the very top of the building. When the last roofing block was in place, the ramps were removed. During the recent dismantling of one of the Nubian temples, sand was found in between the courses of stone, showing that this method of construction had been used.

To erect a building in this way means shifting a colossal amount of sand as well as stone, but the Pharaoh was a god and could command the services of anyone he needed, and during the Inundation there were plenty of peasants who could be usefully employed on building projects until their fields were dry enough to plough.

Erecting an obelisk　　In front of their temples the Egyptians raised obelisks to the honour of the gods. These tall, slim columns of stone, capped by tiny pyramids, were also raised with the help of huge quantities of sand. The illustration on page 45 shows how this was done. Great ramps were constructed to the required height, and the central well was filled with sand. The obelisk was then dragged up the slope, base first, and lowered into position on to the sand. The sand was slowly removed from the bottom, and

A sketch showing building techniques

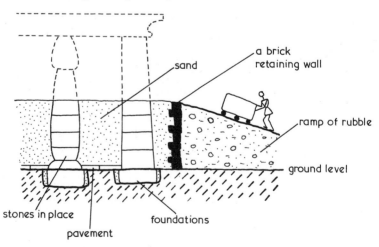

stones in place　　pavement　　foundations

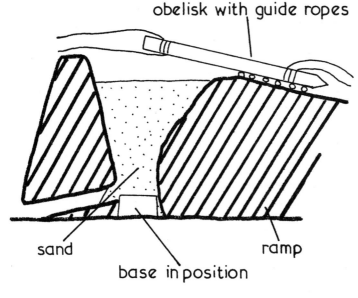

obelisk with guide ropes

A sketch showing
how to raise an
obelisk

sand

ramp

base in position

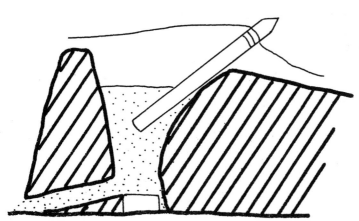

the obelisk sank gently down, being manoeuvered all the way,
until it was in exactly the right position. The ramps were then
removed, and the obelisk was left standing upright. In the
granite quarry at Aswan is an unfinished obelisk. The workmen
had cut and shaped it before they realized that the stone contained a fatal flaw and would break as soon as anyone tried
to raise it. So there it lies to this day, giving archaeologists a

first-rate chance to study the technique of the ancient quarry-men.

When a temple or tomb had been built, or cut into the rock, it was then decorated. Several unfinished tombs show us the stages by which the decoration was applied. First of all the walls were smoothed, and if the decoration was to be painted on, a layer of plaster might be applied. The walls were then divided into squares by snapping pieces of string, soaked in paint, against them. These squares were very important because ancient Egyptian art was subject to very strict rules of proportion. Once the wall was divided into squares the draughtsmen could draw in the scenes to be cut or painted. Here and there a second line in a different ink shows where the master craftsman corrected the lines of the less experienced artists. In the case of a relief, the craftsmen then began cutting out the shapes, while in the case of a painting, the artist blocked in the main areas of colour. Finally, the really expert craftsmen were employed to cut or paint in delicate details.

Tomb
reliefs

APPEARANCE AND DRESS

Archaeology can therefore give quite a clear picture of the homes and the monuments of the ancient Egyptians and can show how they were built; but what did the people themselves look like? The portrait sculpture of the Egyptians was of such a high standard that a good idea of the physical appearance of the Egyptians can be gained by looking at the sculpture galleries of any of the major collections. Also, the practice of mummification has preserved the physical appearance of many Egyptians for study.

In a marvellous climate, such as that enjoyed by Egypt, few clothes are necessary except for the sake of modesty or for decorative purposes. In ancient Egypt children and those engaged in strenuous physical labour dispensed with clothes altogether, and for centuries the fashion for all classes was very simple—a knee-length kilt for men and a straight dress suspended by one or two shoulder straps for the women. In the New Kingdom, however, as part of the general increase in wealth and luxury, fashion for the well-to-do became much more elaborate. Both men and women wore garments of fine linen starched and elaborately pleated. Several garments of cloth have been found stored in chests in tombs, and they bear

Linen

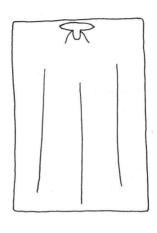

Eighteenth Dynasty costumes

eloquent testimony to the skill of the ancient weavers, for the linen is extremely fine. The illustration on this page shows a man's robe and how this and a woman's dress looked when they were starched and pleated for use. All clothes were made of linen, and white seems to have been the most usual colour, but tomb paintings and models show that other colours were used, and two robes belonging to Tutankhamen were not only brightly coloured but were richly embroidered, as well.

Sculpture and tomb paintings show that elaborate wigs were worn by the aristocracy, and the remains of such wigs have been found in tombs in tall chests specially designed for their storage. Also from tombs come examples of the jewellery worn by both sexes. All the pieces belonging to the wealthy are rich and fine, but none surpasses the taste and craftsmanship of the beautiful jewellery which was buried with some princesses during the Middle Kingdom in their tombs at Lahun and Dahshur.

From the goods buried with their owners in their graves, archaeologists have been able to show that Egyptians of both sexes used eye paint, known as kohl, from the very earliest times. In the Badarian Period malachite, which is green in colour, was used, but later this was replaced by black galena. A

Cosmetics

47

drawing on papyrus in Turin shows a woman painting her lips with a brush, so lipstick of a kind must have been known. In the British Museum there is a relief showing a woman applying rouge to her cheeks.

Egyptian men and women who could afford such luxuries kept their cosmetics in beautifully inlaid boxes specially designed for the purpose. Such boxes contained a mirror, kohl pots and sticks, lip salves and rouge, razors, tweezers, a comb, perfumes, and a variety of scented oils and fats, some to cleanse the body, others to keep the skin soft and to counteract the drying effects of the hot sun.

FURNITURE

Believing firmly that they could literally "take it with them", the Egyptians buried furniture in their tombs for use in the Next World. The most famous examples were, of course, found in the tomb of Tutankhamen, but for beauty and simplicity of line, many people find the furniture buried with Queen Hetepheres, mother of Pharaoh Cheops, more pleasing. Even in the First Dynasty the carpenters were producing rich and beautiful objects, to judge from the remains found in the royal tombs at Sakkara and Abydos.

Furniture like that of the royal tombs of the First Dynasty, of Hetepheres, of Yuya and Tuya (the parents of Queen Tiy, wife of Amenhotep III), and of Tutankhamen show that Egyptian carpenters were extremely skilful and that they understood such techniques as dovetailing and used mortise and tenon joints. The furniture of the wealthy was often overlaid with gold and inlaid with ivory and precious stones.

An Egyptian lady's eye paint and her necklace

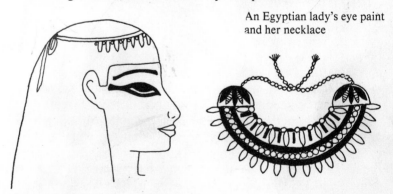

Many carpenter's tools have survived — adzes, axes, bow-drills, chisels, mallets, and saws have been discovered, and tomb paintings, such as those in the tomb of Rekhmire at Thebes, show all these tools being used. The house of a wealthy Egyptian was furnished with low tables, chairs, stools, beds, and chests and baskets of all shapes and sizes for storing things. There were also elaborate stands for lamps and vases. Pottery vessels were used for storage, for cooking, and for eating and drinking, but the wealthy also had beautiful vessels of alabaster, faïence, copper, gold, and silver.

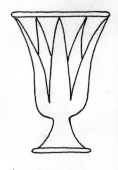

A cup

FOOD

Among the many tombs excavated at Sakkara by Professor W. B. Emery was number 3477, which was constructed in the Second Dynasty. It was not a large or a rich tomb, but it was intact, and when it was entered by the professor and his assistants, there, in the dust on the floor, were the footprints left by the burial party nearly five thousand years before. Among the things left for the old lady who owned the tomb was a meal laid out in dishes. It consisted of bread, porridge, fish, pigeon stew, kidneys, quail, ribs and legs of beef, fruit, cheese and wine, dried up but still recognizable.

Tomb 3477 Sakkara

Egyptian tomb scenes always show the deceased seated in front of a table piled high with food, so we know that besides the dishes left for the old lady in tomb 3477, the Egyptians also enjoyed beer, several sorts of bread and cake, goose and fruit and vegetables of many varieties, including onions, leeks, beans, lentils, lettuce, melons, cucumbers, dates, and sycamore figs.

Archaeology, therefore, has been able to show us a clear picture of the physical appearance of the ancient Egyptians, their clothes, ornaments, furniture, and food, and of the houses in which they lived. Now we must go outside the home and look at the world in which they lived.

AGRICULTURE

The wealth of Egypt was based on its agriculture, and numerous tomb scenes give a vivid picture of what life was like for the peasants. Across the walls of the tombs move the endless rows of slim brown men and women, hard at work in the fields. The pictures shown there are both detailed and accurate.

During the course of many excavations large numbers of agricultural tools have been found, exactly the same as those shown in tomb paintings.

*The farmers'
year*

From Egyptian documents we learn that the year was divided into three seasons, each of four months. The agricultural cycle began with the season of Inundation, lasting from July to November, but the priests and scribes were busy long before the farmer actually began work. The maximum heights of the waters of the Inundation were recorded annually by Nilometers, so that administrative officials could tell in advance whether the harvest was likely to be good or bad. The fields were flooded with the water which carried the rich fertile mud, and no work could be done until the water had subsided and the ground had dried out a little. Then toward the end of October, as the season of Inundation gave way to the season of winter, the season of growth, which lasted from November to March, the peasants faced weeks of weary labour in their fields. First came men with wooden hoes breaking up the clods of earth, preparing the way for the plough. Ploughs were also made of wood, but the share was tipped with copper or bronze. The plough was drawn by a pair of yoked oxen, and a man walked behind, pressing the ploughshare into the soil. Behind the plough moved the sowers, and, after they had scattered the seed, animals were driven over the land to tread in the grain.

Then came a period of waiting while the wheat and barley grew, and the farmers were busy weeding and irrigating their fields. When the wheat was high in the fields, along came the tax collectors and their scribes, measuring, assessing the probable yield of the fields, and fixing the taxes accordingly. In the story known as the "Satire of Trades" a scribe describes several crafts and professions, comparing them all very un-

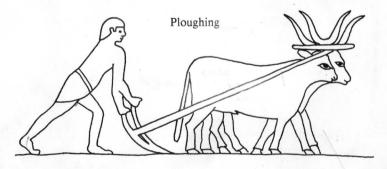

Ploughing

favourably with his own. He is very scathing about the farmers, pointing out that the wretched peasant's crop is at the mercy of snakes, mice, hippopotami, locusts, cattle, sparrows, and thieves, and after all his labours he ends up unable to pay his taxes and he is beaten, while his family is carried off into slavery to meet the taxes.

Harvest came about April. By now it was already getting hot. As the men moved across the fields, swinging their sickles in time to the chant of a singer, those of the women who were not gleaning carried cool water to the fields for the workers.

The summer season lasted from April to June. Once the harvest was in, the grain had to be threshed, winnowed, and then stored in the granaries under the eagle eyes of the ever-present scribes. It was really too hot to do much heavy work after this, but some hard labour had to be done to dig ditches and repair irrigation canals to be ready for the moment when the tears of the goddess Isis, shed in mourning for the death of her husband, Osiris, once more swelled the river and caused the Inundation.

CRAFTSMEN

Like the peasants, the skilled craftsmen left behind their tools, and, of course, some of the things they made have survived to excite our admiration. As with the peasants, the craftsmen and craftswomen can be seen at work in the tomb scenes. Mention has already been made of the tomb of Rekhmire, which has many interesting scenes of craftsmen and craftswomen at work. They are all shown – builders, brickmakers, sculptors, carpenters, jewellers, metal workers, leather workers, weavers, brewers, bakers, and many more. Sometimes pious platitudes exhort the labourers to work harder: "Exert yourself for your dear lord." "O all you gods of this land, bless my powerful master." The ever-watchful scribes scrutinize the products of the craftsmen.

The tomb of Rekhmire

Similar scenes of great interest are to be found in the Old Kingdom tombs of Ti and Mereruka at Sakkara and in the Middle Kingdom tombs at Beni Hasan. On one of their expeditions to the west bank at Thebes, the archaeologists of the Metropolitan Museum of Art, New York, discovered the rock-cut tomb of a nobleman of the Eleventh Dynasty called Meketre. In his tomb he had a whole series of delightful models of men and women at work. These models include a granary

Tomb models of Meketre

51

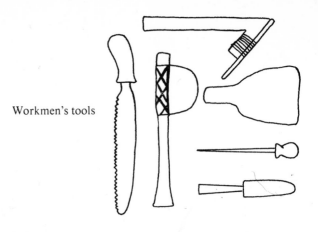

Workmen's tools

with men pouring the grain into the conical storerooms by a hole in the roof, a bakery and brewery, a cattle stall where animals are being fattened for the table, a weaving shed, and several model boats. Some of the little figures had been broken and mended, and it has been suggested that these models were prepared long before Meketre's death and that perhaps his children or grandchildren had used them as toys until they were finally placed in the tomb, where, by magic, they would be living servants to go on catering for their master's needs eternally.

LIFE IN THE MARSHES

Papyrus Among the favourite scenes recorded in tombs are those concerned with life on the river and in the great papyrus marshes along the river banks. The river was rich in fish, and the fishermen sailing up and down in their little papyrus reed boats cast their nets, which, if the tomb paintings are to be believed, never came up empty. For the ancient Egyptian noble the marshes provided recreation, a place where he could fish, catch birds with a throwing stick, or tackle the more exciting and dangerous hippopotamus and crocodile with a harpoon. The papyrus marshes, teeming as they were with water birds, provided not merely sport but a steady food supply, and men are shown netting large numbers of birds for the table. The papyrus plant itself was cut and employed in the manufacture of many articles. The Egyptians' "paper" was made by splitting papyrus stalks, laying them one over the other in a criss-cross

52

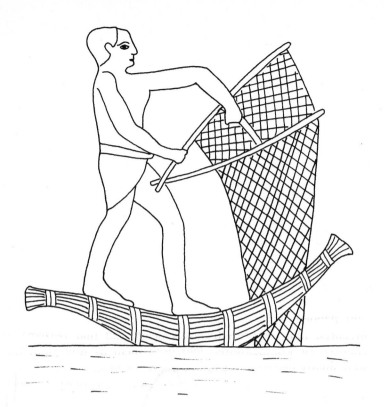

A man fishing from a papyrus boat

pattern, beating them together with mallets, and then drying them so they became welded together into a sheet of paper. Sandals, baskets, roofing materials, and even small boats were also made from reeds.

TRANSPORT

But the Nile did more than provide fish, waterfowl, and papyrus reeds for the Egyptian economy. The river was the great highway of Egypt at a time when roads were of secondary importance. The river was so dominant a feature of the Egyptians' life that it determined their ideas of direction. The words for north and south were "downstream" and "upstream", respectively; and when the Egyptians reached the Euphrates and found that it flowed north–south, instead of south–north like the Nile, they referred to it as the "inverted river". When most people wished to travel any distance in Egypt, they went by water; the river carried soldiers off on

River boats

53

campaigns and embassies on missions; the river brought foreigners and their produce to the wharfs of the capital; the river crossing was part of the last journey made by the dead on their way to their eternal homes in the Western Desert.

The boats of fishermen and the skiffs the aristocracy used when hunting waterfowl were made of bundles of papyrus reeds lashed together, but for large river boats and for sea-going ships, timber was used. Large craft had masts with square sails and a pair of large steering paddles at the stern. When they had no wind or were going against the current, even large vessels had to rely on oars. Model boats were often buried in the tombs of the Middle Kingdom, and several real boats have been discovered, but none so impressive as the great funeral barge of Cheops, found buried near its owner's pyramid at Gizah, ready to ferry the Pharaoh across the sky with the god Re.

Chariots When travelling on land, the Egyptians used donkeys to carry heavy loads for them but had to walk themselves unless they were rich enough to have slaves to carry them around in carrying chairs. From the New Kingdom onward the noblemen also had another method of transport – the horse and chariot. The exact date when horses and chariots were introduced into Egypt is unknown, but it seems to have been sometime during the Second Intermediate Period, though a few horses may have been introduced a little while before that. The small, sway-backed ponies were of little use for riding, though occasionally army scouts and grooms are shown riding and exercising horses. The animals' real job was to draw chariots. The chariots themselves were light, wooden structures with leather and metal harness, but royal chariots were elaborately decorated and overlaid in gold. Chariots could hold only two passengers

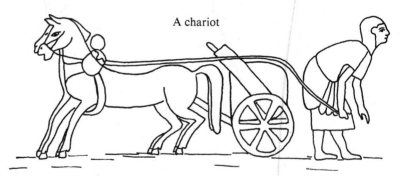

A chariot

and were drawn by two horses. Many pictures of chariots have survived, and so have some actual chariots, including the one which belonged to Tutankhamen. In peace time the nobility hunted desert game from their chariots, and in time of war they provided the élite corps of the army.

THE ARMY

In the earliest times, before the introduction of the horse, the Egyptian army consisted only of infantry. In the reign of Ramesses II the army was composed of four divisions, named for the gods Amen, Ptah, Re, and Sutekh, whose standards were carried into battle. Documents and reliefs, such as those describing the wars of Ramesses II against the Hittites, show that on campaign an Egyptian camp was a well-organized place. It is also likely that several agreeable luxuries were to be found in the officers' tents. Tutankhamen, for example, besides folding stools, possessed a camp bed, which could be folded up into a third of its length to make it easier to transport.

Our knowledge of ancient Egyptian weapons comes from battle scenes in tombs and on monuments and, of course, from the actual weapons themselves, which have been found buried with their owners. In the Old and Middle Kingdoms the warriors seem to have worn little or no body armour and no helmets, but in New Kingdom reliefs soldiers are shown in helmets and wearing armour, which appears to have been made of leather reinforced with metal scales. Tutankhamen's protective corselet had golden scales. The soldiers had a variety of weapons to choose from – mace, axe, sword, dagger, spear, and bow and arrow, and a shield for protection.

During the Middle Kingdom the Egyptians conquered Nubia and built a string of forts along the river from which they dominated the countryside. The recent excavations in Nubia, prior to the flooding of the area by the waters of the Aswan Dam, have revealed that these forts, such as those at Buhen and Mirgissa, were impressive structures by any standard, comparable in their defensive strength to the best strongholds built in Europe in medieval times. At Buhen, for example, Professor W. B. Emery and his assistants on the Egypt Exploration Society's expedition found that the main walls of the fort measured 170 by 150 metres. The walls were at least 10 metres high and over 5 metres thick. The fort was built by the river,

The great fort of Buhen

55

Twelfth Dynasty warriors

and the most elaborate defences faced the desert, so the enemy
was obviously expected to attack from that direction.

To capture Buhen the enemy had first to advance across the
open desert and then descend into a deep ditch, while con-
stantly under fire from the ramparts above. They then had to
scale the side of the ditch and capture the lower ramparts. Even
if they got this far, the attackers had several more hazards to
face. Once the lower ramparts were taken, they would find
themselves in a narrow corridor between the lower ramparts
and the main walls of the fortress, and the defenders could pour
arrows and rocks down on them. Towers projected from the
main wall every few metres, and these all had rows of triple
arrow slits to enable the defenders to fire in any direction. The
crossfire from these towers could protect the whole wall. Apart
from the two water gates, the only entrance to Buhen was the
great West Gate. If the attackers got through the great wooden
doors, they found themselves in an enclosed space with the
defenders hurling missiles down on them. In the north of Egypt
there was another string of forts, referred to in literature as
"The Walls of the Prince". These were built across the eastern
Delta's frontier with Sinai to keep out marauding desert
nomads.

A find by an American team of archaeologists shed an interesting ray of light on one ancient battle. After the period of
internal strife and weakness known as the First Intermediate
Period, the ruler of Thebes, Nebhepetre Mentuhotep, swept
56 northward against his rival and successfully brought all Egypt

A Pharaoh's Double Crown and Blue War Helmet

under his rule. In March, 1923, the archaeologists excavating near his mortuary temple at Deir el Bahari found a tomb in the nearby cliffs which contained the bodies of sixty or so soldiers of this Pharaoh. When the bodies were examined, certain facts emerged which enabled the excavators to make the following deductions. The injuries sustained by these long-dead warriors showed that they had been wounded by arrows and by missiles, such as stones, being hurled down upon them. Further, there were no slashes from sword or axe, such as would have occurred during a hand-to-hand fight, so it could be assumed that the men had fallen while besieging a citadel. It was also clear, upon examination, that several men had not expired from these wounds but from being clubbed to death. It would seem that they had attacked a city and had been driven back. Those who were too badly wounded to flee were dispatched by the enemy and left lying in the sand, where kites and vultures started pecking the bodies. Later the army of Mentuhotep returned and, having defeated the enemy, gathered the remains of their fallen comrades for burial. The battle must have been an important one, perhaps the final battle that won Mentuhotep mastery over the Two Kingdoms, for he buried these soldiers near the site of his own mortuary temple, which was a great honour.

The slain soldiers of Nebhepetre

TRADE

From actual objects found, from tomb paintings, and from literary sources we know that many foreign articles and

57

materials found their way into Egypt either as trade, or loot, or as tribute.

Within the boundaries of Egypt there were plentiful supplies of stone for building – limestone, sandstone, and granite. The rarer, more beautiful stones – alabaster, basalt, breccia, marble, porphyry, quartzite, and schist – which were used to make luxury articles, were also all to be found in Egypt, and in fact the only stone that was regularly supplied from outside was diorite. This seems to have been fetched from a quarry in the Western Desert about 64 km northwest of Abu Simbel, in Nubia. Stone was therefore in plentiful supply, but Egypt was poorly provided by nature with large trees. The native timbers most commonly employed by Egyptian carpenters were acacia, sycamore, fig, and tamarisk, though palm trees, persea, and willow were also used. However, Egypt had to look outside her boundaries for trees that could provide long, high-grade planks for large ships, buildings, and the best furniture and coffins.

Cedars of Lebanon "And Solomon sent to Huram the king of Tyre, saying, As thou didst deal with David my father, and didst send him cedars to build him an house to dwell therein, even so deal with me" (2 Chronicles 2:3). In ancient times the Lebanon was the chief source of timber for all the Near Eastern countries. Some 1,800 years before Solomon, Sneferu, the first king of Egypt's Fourth Dynasty, recorded that a trading expedition had brought home forty ships laden with timber. The trade with the Lebanon can be traced back a long way before Sneferu, however, for cedarwood was found on a site dated to the Badarian Period.

Metal working Copper, one of the first metals to be used by the Egyptians, was to be found in the Eastern Desert, and the people of the Badarian Period probably mined it there, but, by the Third Dynasty, mines were being worked in the Sinai Peninsula, where there are rock-cut scenes showing the Pharaohs slaying the local inhabitants. Later, however, by the Twelfth Dynasty, friendly relations had been established with the local people, and they joined the Egyptians in their copper-mining enterprises. The copper was used for tools, weapons, jewellery, statues, and eating and drinking vessels.

Bronze, which is an alloy of copper and tin, was known in Egypt from the Old Kingdom onward, but it was not until the 58 Middle Kingdom, about 2000 B.C., that it became common.

Toilet articles

Tin had to be imported into Egypt, but the source has been hotly disputed and is still uncertain. Claims have been made for Europe, Africa, and Asia respectively as being the place where tin was first discovered. In his invaluable book *Ancient Egyptian Materials and Industries*, Alfred Lucas favours Asia and suggests Persia as a possible source.

Gold, used for jewellery from the earliest times, was mined in the Eastern Desert, but Nubia was the greatest producer of gold, and it was for this reason that the Pharaohs of the Middle Kingdom thought it worth their while to conquer and rule there. Though gold was plentiful, silver was not found in Egypt and had to be imported from Syria. It was so rare that in some periods it was held to be more valuable than gold.

Meteoric iron was fashioned into beads at a very early period, but it could only be shaped by hammering. To cast iron like copper and bronze, very high temperatures were required, which these ancient smiths could not achieve. Iron was so rare that even Tutankhamen possessed only a dagger, a miniature headrest, an amulet, and a few ritual implements made of iron. It was not until the Twenty-fifth Dynasy (751–664 B.C.) that iron became common in Egypt.

So far, only raw materials have been dealt with, but many other products were also imported to Egypt. Syria and Crete, for example, sent luxury manufactured goods to Egypt, and the Sinai–Palestine area was a source of slaves, some of them being captured on campaigns, others being sold by their own people as part of their regular trading goods: "Then there passed by Midianites, merchantmen; and they drew and lifted up Joseph out of the pit, and sold Joseph to the Ishmaelites for twenty pieces of silver: and they brought Joseph into Egypt" (Genesis 37:28).

Besides copper, the mines of Sinai supplied the Egyptians with turquoise, but the source of lapis lazuli was much farther away, probably in Afghanistan. Punt supplied Egypt with incense, and from Nubia and Kush, besides gold, came ebony, ivory, slaves, ostrich feathers, animal skins, and animals themselves.

Into Egypt, therefore, especially during the triumphant days of the New Kingdom, flowed riches from all over the known world. The Pharaohs did not suffer from an excess of modesty, so on their monuments all goods acquired by trade were usually entered as tribute sent by humble foreigners to the Ruler of the Two Lands.

MEDICINE

When a people buries its dead without cremating them, it is unintentionally providing much valuable information for the archaeologists of the future. The Egyptians, of course, are especially famous for their custom of mummification. Palaeo-pathologists have examined many ancient Egyptian mummies and have gathered much interesting information about disease in Pharaonic times. Of course, many diseases cannot be traced at this distance in time, but others can. For example, bones of Egyptian mummies have revealed that the Egyptians suffered from arthritis, just as many unfortunate people do today. Also, the presence of tuberculosis has been detected in the bones of mummies, and the mummy of the Pharaoh Siptah revealed that he had a club foot. Then, again, it has been found that the Egyptians suffered from bilharzia, which is a curse even today and which is still endemic in widespread areas of the African continent. An examination of the teeth of mummies has shown that in ancient times people were vulnerable to tooth decay, 60 abscesses, and pyorrhoea, just as we are now.

From the bodies of long-dead Egyptians we can therefore learn a good deal about their ailments, and we can deduce that they were competent to do such things as set broken bones, but a large number of pathetically small corpses also reveals that there was a high infant mortality rate. Classical writers recorded that the Egyptian doctors were famous throughout the Mediterranean world and that many were specialists, each treating one organ of the body only. Egyptian literary sources tell us rather more. Several medical textbooks have survived, the best known being the Ebers Papyrus, the Hearst Papyrus, the Edwin Smith Papyrus, and the Kahun Papyrus. From these it would seem that, although prayers and magic spells played a part in Egyptian medicine, as it did in the medicine of most countries until the eighteenth century of our era, the Egyptian doctors nevertheless also practised a rational examination, diagnosis, and treatment of disease. It is most unfortunate that the English meanings of most of the names of herbs and drugs referred to in prescriptions are not known, so that it is not possible to say just how effective some of their remedies were.

The medical Papyri

MUMMIFICATION AND FUNERALS
When medical remedies failed and a man or woman died, he or she was held to have passed from the kingdom of the living into

A mummy wrapped ready for burial and its four canopic jars

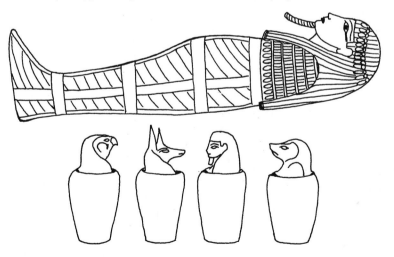

the kingdom of Osiris, the god of the dead. With the help of documents and tomb paintings, archaeologists have been able to reconstruct the funeral ceremonies and burial equipment provided for a wealthy Egyptian.

Mummification   Once a nobleman had died, his body was handed over to the priests and embalmers. When fully developed, as it was by the Eighteenth Dynasty, the process of embalming was a long and complicated one, performed as a religious rite to the accompaniment of ritual prayers. First the brain was removed, and the heart and contents of the abdominal cavity. The body was washed out and the interior packed with linen or sawdust, and possibly spices, as well. The body was then placed in a bath of natron, which acted as a drying agent. It was once thought that the natron was in a liquid form, but the experiments of Alfred Lucas suggest that solid natron was packed around the body. The corpse lay in its natron bath for seventy days; then it was taken out, jewellery was put on it, gold protective sheaths were put over the finger and toenails, and golden sandals were put on its feet. The heart was replaced by a special amulet known as a heart scarab. The body was then wrapped in yards of bandages, and protective amulets were slipped in among the bandages. A portrait mask was put over the head and shoulders, and the mummy was then placed in its anthropoid (human-shaped) coffin. These coffins were usually made of wood and were
A shwabti   decorated with gold leaf if the owner was rich. The burial of Tutankhamen shows that kings had a series of coffins which fitted one within the other like a nest of Chinese boxes, and that the innermost coffin was solid gold.

The funeral procession of a nobleman of the New Kingdom at Thebes must have been a very impressive affair. The column was headed by priests leading bulls that were destined for sacrifice. Then came all the dead man's belongings that were to be packed into the tomb—furniture of all kinds, his gaming board, chariot, clothes, jewels, food and drink, and also divine statues and amulets, which were to help his *ka* (soul) in its journey across the Lily Lake to the Other World, where many dangers awaited the spirit unless it knew the correct spells. A man who could afford it had a large roll of papyrus inscribed with all the magic formulae that his *ka* was likely to need.

People of all classes included *shwabtis* among their grave
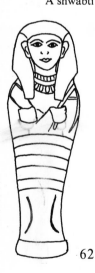
62   goods. A *shwabti* is a small mummy-shaped figure made of

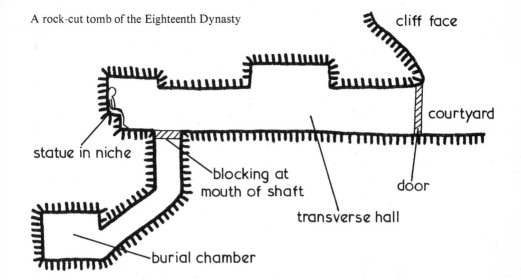

A rock-cut tomb of the Eighteenth Dynasty

cliff face

courtyard

statue in niche

blocking at
mouth of shaft

door

transverse hall

burial chamber

wood, faïence, or stone, and it carries tools, usually a hoe and a seed bag. Across the middle of the *shwabti* a spell was written. The idea was that when the dead man was called by Osiris, the King of the Dead, to do some hard manual work such as digging, the magic *shwabti* figure would come to life and do the required task. In the Late Period, some tombs contained boxes with over three hundred small *shwabtis* in them, presumably so that the owner would have a different labourer available for every day of the year.

Statues of the dead man might also be carried in the funeral procession, but there was usually a life-sized statue already in place in the tomb. If, by chance, the mummy of the dead man was destroyed, the *ka* would still be able to find a resting place in the statue.

Behind the offering bearers came more priests, the bier on which the mummy was carried, and the canopic chest, in which were stored the organs that had been removed from the body. The bier was surrounded by professional women mourners, who wept and wailed during the whole journey. Behind the bier followed the deceased's family and retainers. The whole procession left the city, was ferried over the Nile, and re-formed on the west bank, where it continued its journey to the necropolis. At the tomb the most important ceremony of all, that of "The

"The Opening of the Mouth"

63

Opening of the Mouth", was performed. This ceremony was supposed to give the corpse the use of its faculties again so that it could "live" in the Other World. A sacrifice was made to the dead man's spirit, and the coffin was finally lowered into the stone sarcophagus, the lid was placed over it, and the burial party withdrew. As the priests left, they brushed away their footprints, but sometimes they missed one, and these have survived in a few intact tombs. In others the marks of the brush can still be clearly seen, and twigs that dropped out of the brushes have been found.

When these ceremonies were over, the mourners held a funeral feast, and from then on it was the duty of the dead man's son to keep his father's tomb supplied with fresh offerings. The Egyptians believed that, just as once the god Osiris had been resurrected by his sister-wife, Isis, after he had been *The Day of* murdered by his wicked brother, Set, so, too, would they live *Judgement* again in the Next World. If they had lived virtuous lives and their souls passed the test of being weighed in the Scales of Truth, then they would enjoy eternal bliss. A bad life and a soul heavy with sin meant punishment in the Hereafter.

RELIGION

Sacred From Greek writers such as Herodotus and Diodorus we learn
animals that the Egyptians had the reputation of being extremely pious, though many visitors in the Late Period found the animal cults hard to understand. In the early days Egyptians did not worship whole species of animals as they did later, but they did believe that the gods chose to manifest themselves in a single animal of a certain species. Thus the Apis bull, identified by special markings, was kept at Memphis and was considered sacred because the spirit of the god Ptah was incarnate in it. That from Predynastic times the Egyptians believed that their gods could manifest themselves in animals is shown by amulets which have been discovered, such as those in the shape of a hawk, the emblem of Horus, the sky god.

Religion undoubtedly played an important role in Egyptian life, offering comfort to the distressed and an escape from the monotony of hard work. Every site excavated in Egypt seems to yield large numbers of amulets made of everything from gold and semi-precious stones to cheap blue-green faïence,
64   showing that both rich and poor shared a faith in the protective

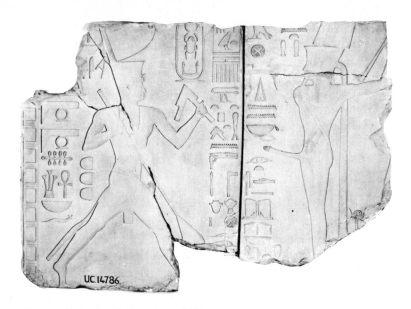

Senusret I dancing before the god Min

powers of the emblems of their favourite deities. Most houses
probably also possessed a small shrine where a statue of a
divinity or an amulet could be kept. There were many temples
in Egypt, and these could vary in size from the group of
immense buildings at Karnak to more modest structures such
as the workmen's temple at Deir el Medineh, and to very small
village shrines. One feature that they all had in common, *Temples*
however, was that the general public was excluded. Around the
whole temple area was a high wall, pierced by a single gate,
giving the whole place the aspect of a fortress. Within the inner
wall of a large temple were the administrative buildings, and in
the centre was the temple proper. The temple had only one
entrance, between two great pylons (towers). In front of the
pylons would stand the obelisks, together with flagpoles and
statues of the king. Passing through the pylons the purified
priests crossed one or more open courtyards into the temple
building, which usually consisted of a great columned hall, an
ante-chamber and side chambers, and the sanctuary. Very little
light entered from the small, high windows, and as one
approached the sanctuary in the innermost part of the temple,
the floor level was raised and the ceilings were built lower so   65

the sense of awe and mystery was increased as one came nearer to the divinity. The statue of the god or goddess was kept in this sanctuary, from which light, impurity, and evil were firmly excluded. As the Pharaoh in his palace was protected from the gaze of the vulgar, whose impurity might contaminate him and make him ritually impure, so were the gods protected. On great feast days, however, the statue of the deity would be taken from the temple, placed in a sacred bark (boat), and carried on the shoulders of the priests through the streets so that the faithful might worship. At Luxor today the relics of the holy Sheik Abu Haggag are carried through the streets at his festival, just as once Amen-Re, king of the gods, was carried forth at the Feast of Opet.

The oracle   It might be thought that the gods, shut away in their dark temples, would seem remote and unsympathetic beings, but the documents show that Egyptians of all classes from the Pharaoh downward made a habit of appealing to the oracle of the god at their local temple whenever a difficult decision had to be reached. The questions were written down on papyrus or on broken pieces of pottery and taken to the god by the priests. Many of these pleas have been found during the excavation of several temples. "Whom should I choose to be the next High Priest?" "Is this man a thief?" "Shall I plough my field to-morrow?" No query was too great or too small to receive the attention of the oracle. Sometimes the answer was given by the god's statue moving its head or arm (carefully manipulated by the High Priest, presumably), but on other occasions the god's statue might, while being carried in procession, suddenly become so heavy that the priests could carry it no farther. Tuthmosis III records that this was how the god Amen-Re chose him to be king. Texts describing the interpretation of dreams have also been found by archaeologists. A dream might contain an omen, the answer to a prayer, or the diagnosis of an illness, so careful interpretation was needed.

Along with oracles and dream interpretations, the documents have also preserved for us such things as the form of ritual to be performed at morning and evening services, prayers, spells, and the names of the gods and the tales of their exploits, so that our knowledge of the Egyptian religion has been greatly increased by the ability to read hieroglyphs.

Archaeologists can learn a lot about a people from their

houses and their graves, but because we can read hieroglyphs and because the Egyptians carved on stone and wrote on papyrus, a substance which survives well in the Egyptian climate, we can learn much more about them. From historical records on their monuments and from official documents we can deduce the details of their political and dynastic struggles, we can come to appreciate a little the depth of their religious beliefs, their medical knowledge, and their legal and administrative systems, but we are also privileged to read their letters, their accounts, their stories, and their love songs, and so to go a little way toward understanding their thoughts.

CHAPTER FOUR

Important Discoveries

In the course of the last chapter we examined several aspects of life in ancient Egypt as it has been revealed by archaeologists, and saw how much has also been found out from tomb paintings and inscriptions. In this chapter we are going to look at certain specific excavations and documents. They have been chosen either because they show how important an individual excavation can be in altering the known history of a given period or because they illustrate an interesting aspect of the archaeologist's work.

CHRONOLOGY, THE TURIN CANON, AND CARBON 14

An archaeologist who is excavating the remains of an "historic", literate people like the ancient Egyptians, who had worked out a calendar and gave dates to the reigns of each king, can often date his site very accurately to within a few years. The archaeologist dealing with a "prehistoric" people who left no written documents, or with a people whose script cannot yet be read, has to resort to methods of detection.

Sequence dating Let us begin with the example of a hypothetical village settlement. A group of people build a village for themselves on a new site. As time passes, houses fall into disrepair and are pulled down, and new ones are then built on top of the rubble of the old. In the course of several centuries quite a mound of debris may accumulate above the ground level of the original settlement. It is quite obvious that when this mound is excavated archaeologists are going to find the remains left by the most recent inhabitants on the top of the mound and the remains left by the earliest inhabitants at the bottom. A careful study of the objects of the various stratified layers will show how tastes and styles changed during the course of the settlement's history. Let us suppose that when the village was built pottery of a type we will call "A" was popular. Later the shape begins to change till

68

it develops into a new type, "B", and later still an entirely new type, "C", is introduced, and so on. Because the site is stratified, and because the new and old styles of pottery overlap at times, a sequence of pottery, "A", "B", "C", can be built up. This "sequence dating" method was first developed by Sir W. M. Flinders Petrie and set out in his publication of *Diospolis Parva* in 1901.

The sequence dating system must be based on a class of objects which will be found in a plentiful supply on most sites or it will not work properly. Archaeologists in Egypt usually use pottery, because there is always plenty to be found on Egyptian sites. Moreover, it breaks easily and is not valuable, so it is unlikely to be passed on from one generation to the next. There is little danger, therefore, that it will turn up in a layer formed long after the pot was originally made. Sequence dating was the method Petrie used to establish the Badarian–Amratian–Gerzean sequence of Egypt's Predynastic, non-literate cultures. The sequence dating method, however, can only indicate the development in style of any class of objects. It cannot give the date in years that the objects were made. To find an accurate date the archaeologist needs inscribed material. Egyptologists have been able to establish many dates with a fair degree of accuracy. For example, in some documents there are records of the movements of certain stars, such as the "Dog Star", Sirius, which the Egyptians called "Sothis". Because Sirius was recorded as being in a certain quarter of the heavens on a known day in the seventh year of the reign of the Pharaoh Sesostris III, astronomers and archaeologists have been able to calculate that the Twelfth Egyptian Dynasty began in 1991 B.C.

We must now deal briefly with one of the greatest tragedies of Egyptology. In the early years of the last century Bernadino Drovetti, the French Consul General, acquired the papyrus now known as the Turin Canon of Kings. This absolutely unique and irreplaceable papyrus, written in the reign of Ramesses II, contained a list of all the previous kings of Egypt, together with the lengths of their reigns. The papyrus was eventually given to the Turin Museum, and when it was examined, it was discovered that, although it had been almost intact when originally found, on one stage of its journey to Turin it had been put in a box without proper protective packing. It arrived in fragments.

Foreign juglets found in Egypt

Hieroglyphs saying
King of Upper and
Lower Egypt

Years of patient work followed, with scholars trying to fit pieces of the papyrus back together again and to reconstruct the missing parts. They have now been able to glean enough information from the Turin Canon to calculate that Egypt's First Dynasty began in about 3100 B.C., a figure that is accurate to within a few years. The Egyptian chronology is the best available for the Near East, and archaeologists working throughout the area base their dates upon those of Egypt. Once Egyptian objects are found abroad or foreign goods are found in an Egyptian grave, a link has been established between the two cultures, and what is called "cross dating" can take place.

Cross dating For example, in Crete, Egyptian objects were found in association with pottery of the Cretan Middle Minoan III Period, while in the tombs of Rekhmire and Useramen at Thebes there are pictures of Keftiu (Minoan) envoys bringing gifts to the Pharaohs. These gifts can be identified as being metal versions of pottery vessels produced in Crete and in Mycenae, in Greece, during their Late Minoan II and Late Helladic II periods.

During the last few years physicists and archaeologists have been co-operating in order to find new and more accurate dating techniques. One field of research that has received a good deal *Carbon 14* of publicity is the carbon 14 process, which was first discovered in 1950 by Professor W. F. Libby of the University of California. The carbon 14 process is used to date wooden objects and plants, such as reeds and flax, from ancient sites. When a plant is growing, it absorbs carbon, including radioactive carbon (carbon 14), from the air. When the plant dies, it stops taking in carbon 14 and starts losing it. It was first thought that ancient plants lost their carbon 14 at a slow, steady rate, the same amount each year, so that by measuring the amount left, say, in a piece of ancient wood, it would be possible to work out how many years ago the tree was cut down.

Archaeologists began to send samples, particularly of ancient wood, from their excavations to laboratories, where physicists measured the amount of carbon 14 left in each specimen and told the archaeologists when they thought each tree had been cut down. This was, of course, very important for dating prehistoric sites, where there was no written evidence to help the archaeologists to date their finds.

70 Some scholars, however, particularly Egyptologists, were

worried because the carbon 14 dates did not fit in with the chronologies already worked out by cross dating (see page 70). In the end it was decided to conduct an experiment to see just how well the carbon 14 dates for Egyptian material would agree with the dates worked out by the archaeologists and astronomers. Samples of wood, reeds, and linen were collected from well-dated Egyptian sites, and a series of carbon 14 dates was produced for them. It was discovered that although some of the more recent dates agreed exactly, by the time of the First Dynasty (*circa* 3100 B.C.) there was a difference of up to five hundred years between the dates worked out by the archaeologists and the carbon 14 dates. It is now realized that, for various reasons, carbon 14 is not lost at a steady rate each year, but that more has been lost at some periods than at others. When physicists have worked out a table of adjustments, the carbon 14 process should give accurate dates for sites all over the world. It is an extremely useful discovery, and material from Egyptian sites has been valuable in checking its accuracy.

WHERE ARE THE ROYAL TOMBS OF THE FIRST DYNASTY?

Abydos was the Holy City of ancient Egypt, the place where it was believed that the god Osiris was buried. When Sir W. M. Flinders Petrie began his famous excavation there at the end of the last century, he discovered a series of mud-brick rectangular structures known as *mastabas*.

Petrie at Abydos

From inscriptions in primitive hieroglyphs he was able to allot mastabas to individual kings of the First Dynasty. Each mastaba covered a burial chamber. To judge from the remains of furniture, jewellery, and stone pottery vessels found in them, they had been well stocked with provisions for the Next World, and around each mastaba was a series of smaller tombs containing the burials of the kings' servants and courtiers. Petrie assumed that he had found the last resting place of the kings of the First Dynasty, and for forty years no one in the archaeological world saw any reason to disagree. Then in 1936 W. B. Emery began work on the Archaic Necropolis at Sakkara, and the whole question was thrown back into the melting pot once more.

At Sakkara, which is just north of Memphis, the new capital

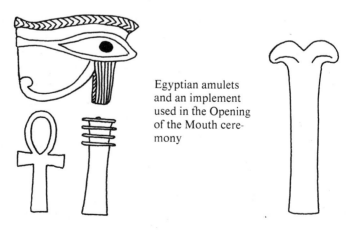

A section of a wall showing the panels and recesses of the "Palace Façade" style

Evidence of Sakkara
city founded by Menes after his Unification of the Two Lands in about 3100 B.C., Professor Emery also discovered a whole series of mastaba tombs containing beautiful tomb furniture, some of which was inscribed with the names of First Dynasty kings. Whereas the Abydos tombs had straight sides, the walls of the Sakkara tombs were elaborately panelled and recessed, in a style which is known as a "palace façade". As at Abydos, the Sakkara tombs were surrounded by the subsidiary burials of servants who, it seems, were sent to join their royal masters in the Other World. (The practice of sacrificing the servants of dead monarchs appears to have died out in Egypt by the end of the First Dynasty.)

Beautiful grave goods had been buried in the Sakkara mastabas, just as they had been at Abydos, and on the north side of Mastaba 3357, the tomb of Hor-aha, the remains of a whole model estate were found, together with the grave of a boat, which had been buried so that Hor-aha could sail with the sun god across the sky. It has been suggested that the Sakkara tombs belonged to courtiers, but they were all larger than those

Egyptian amulets and an implement used in the Opening of the Mouth ceremony

72

at Abydos. To take one example, the tomb of Zer at Abydos was about 21·5 by 20 metres, while the tomb bearing his name at Sakkara was approximately 41 by 15 metres. It does not seem very likely that a god-king would tolerate courtiers having a more splendid tomb than he had himself!

So it would seem that the kings of the First Dynasty had two tombs. This is not really as silly as it sounds, for it must be remembered that Egypt was two kingdoms, united only in the person of the ruler. It would seem that the first kings of a united land were buried near their new capital but also provided themselves with a fully equipped cenotaph at the burial place of their ancestors, Abydos.

THE TOMB OF HETEPHERES

In February, 1925, the Harvard–Boston Expedition, under the direction of Dr. George Reisner, was excavating at Gizah, near the pyramid of Cheops. Under a pavement the expedition found the mouth of a vertical shaft that had been filled with stone blocks. A little way down, the blocks gave way to less well-cut stone and rubble. About 9 metres down, the excavators found a side chamber in which were two jars of beer and part of an ox, sacrificed to the *ka* of the owner of the tomb. Over 12 metres down, they came across fragments of pottery and copper, and at 21·3 metres yet more pottery was discovered. Finally, some 26 metres below the pavement where the shaft had started, the workmen found their way blocked with masonry. When this was removed, the expedition could see below them the remains of a rich burial.

It took months to clear the burial chamber and an even longer period of painstaking work to reconstruct the beautiful furniture which is now on display in the Cairo Museum. Inscriptions revealed that the owner of the tomb was Queen Hetepheres, wife of the Pharaoh Sneferu and mother of the Pharaoh Cheops, who built the Great Pyramid at Gizah. Her tomb furniture included her bed, chair, canopy, chest, and carrying chair; a box containing silver anklets; and her gold and copper vessels and toilet articles. Besides all this, there were, of course, the queen's canopic chest and her alabaster sarcophagus.

When the excited archaeologists opened the sarcophagus, a nasty shock awaited them – it was empty. They had found an

Mother of the King of Upper and Lower Egypt

73

intact tomb, yet the body had disappeared. Reisner, reviewing his evidence, suggested the following solution.

When Hetepheres died, she was buried, as might be expected, near the pyramid of her husband, Sneferu, at Dahshur, but when Cheops came to the throne, he decided to build his pyramid at Gizah. This probably meant that the Dahshur necropolis was less strictly guarded than before, and one night thieves broke into the tomb of Hetepheres. The richest jewels were always on the body, so they attacked the sarcophagus first, ripping away bandages and destroying the mummy in their haste. Perhaps they were disturbed; at any rate, they did no more damage.

An ancient
mystery
Cheops, furious that his mother's grave had been violated, ordered an investigation to be made and decided that his mother's body and goods should be transferred to the comparative safety of Gizah. Did Cheops ever know his mother's body was missing? Possibly not. God-kings have notoriously unpredictable tempers. Perhaps the unfortunate official in charge of the whole operation was too afraid to tell the king, in which case the reburial was probably arranged with frantic haste, lest the dreadful secret leak out.

A deep shaft was cut hastily and a chamber was prepared at the bottom, but no attempt was made to smooth the walls as was usually done. The sarcophagus and furniture were bundled into the chamber, the chamber entrance was sealed, and the work of filling in the shaft commenced. It was found that they had forgotten to put the Queen's pottery vessels in the chamber, so these were placed in the shaft and covered with the filling. In their haste the workmen let rubbish fall into the shaft and left their tools behind, but there was no going back. A sacrifice was made to the Queen's *ka*, the shaft was finally blocked, and later a pavement was laid over it, concealing the entrance for 4,500 years. If this reconstruction by Reisner is correct, one can almost hear the sigh of relief of the official in charge as the final block of stone was lowered into place!

THE BUHEN COPPER TOWN AND THE BUHEN HORSE
One day in 1960 Mrs. W. B. Emery, wife of Professor Emery, was exercising her dogs in the desert behind her husband's excavations of the great fort at Buhen in Nubia. On the surface
74 of the desert she found pieces of red pottery and fragments of

copper, which she took back to the dig house. Investigation on the site of her find added a whole new chapter to the history of Nubia.

The pottery was of a very distinctive type known as Meydum ware, which belongs to the Egyptian Old Kingdom, and clay jar sealings on the site were inscribed with the names of Old Kingdom Pharaohs. Excavation revealed a much denuded townsite, which had sheltered behind defensive walls about two metres thick.

This Old Kingdom town at Buhen, therefore, revealed that the Egyptians were making attempts at colonization in Nubia several hundred years earlier than anyone had hitherto suspected.

During the Second Intermediate Period the great forts of Nubia were abandoned by the Egyptians but were rebuilt in a modified form during the New Kingdom, when the Pharaohs of the Eighteenth Dynasty reasserted their control over the area.

In Buhen fort, under a New Kingdom layer of brickwork was a stratified deposit, over a metre deep, which included the debris caused by the destruction of the Middle Kingdom fortifications in about 1675 B.C. Under this debris, at the Middle Kingdom level, was the skeleton of a horse. It has already been pointed out that the horse is thought to have been introduced into Egypt just prior to the beginning of the Eighteenth Dynasty by the Hyksos. It was therefore a great surprise to find the skeleton of a horse at Buhen at a level dated to nearly two hundred years before they were supposed to have arrived in Egypt.

The skeleton was identified as probably male and aged about *A pet horse* nineteen years. The horse was known in Mesopotamia several hundred years before it was introduced into Egypt. Did an Egyptian official of the Middle Kingdom travel to Syria or Mesopotamia and bring back the strange animal as a pet? If so, he was so attached to it that, when duty took the master to Nubia, the horse went too.

THE AMARNA TABLETS
Mention has already been made on page 18 of the woman who went looking for fertilizer and found the Foreign Office of a Pharaoh. The letters are written on clay tablets, and they have suffered a good deal from being thrown into a sack and

A portrait head of a Middle Kingdom Pharaoh

bumped about on their way to a dealer, but enough remains to allow us a fascinating glimpse into the diplomatic world in 1350 B.C.

Palestine and Syria during the Eighteenth and Nineteenth Dynasties of Egypt were ruled by numerous petty, competing princelings, some under the patronage of Egypt, others looking north to the Hittites of Anatolia for protection. While Egypt was ruled by strong, active warriors, like Tuthmosis III and Amenhotep II, the balance was precariously maintained, but during the last years of the reign of Amenhotep III and under his son Akhenaten, the situation rapidily deteriorated.

Shubilulliuma, King of the Hittites, wanted to expand his empire in Syria at the expense of Egypt but was not prepared to risk an open conflict with the Pharaohs. In the persons of Abdu-Ashirta and his son Aziru, rulers of the small principality of Amor, the wily Hittite found the perfect tools. While writing flattering and servile letters to the Pharaoh, these two traitors were busy annexing land that belonged to loyal vassals of Egypt. The coastal cities, so vital to Egypt's prosperity, fell one after the other to Aziru till Byblos alone was left. Its prince, Ribaddi, sent desperate pleas for help to Egypt, but he was ignored. Byblos fell to Aziru. One can only hope that Ribaddi's end was a mercifully quick one.

From Jerusalem the Egyptian deputy Abdu-Heba also wrote begging for help. He was being plagued by the Habiru, or Sagaz ("cut-throats"), an amalgamation of various tribes, probably, as the name "Habiru" suggests, including peoples of Hebrew speech and customs. Be that as it may, the southern part of Egypt's empire began to disintegrate just as the northern part was doing.

It may be wondered what sort of a man Akhenaten was, sitting safely in Egypt and leaving his vassals to die unaided. Perhaps he was a pacifist, as some scholars have suggested, or perhaps there was someone in his Foreign Office who took care that the truth did not reach the Pharaoh. We do not know. Scenes in the tomb which General Horemheb prepared for himself before he became Pharaoh suggest that he made some efforts which prevented a complete collapse of Egypt's fortunes abroad. His reign as Pharaoh seems to have been dedicated to clearing up the confusion left by, and eradicating all traces of, Akhenaten's reign. After Horemheb's reign of nearly thirty

A man and his wife of the late
Eighteenth Dynasty

years, his successors, Seti I and Ramesses II, were in a strong enough position to carry out vigorous campaigns in Palestine and Syria.

The woman with her sack of unexciting-looking clay tablets, therefore, made a fascinating contribution to the history of the whole of the Near East, though she was an archaeologist by accident rather than design.

THE MYSTERIOUS BODY IN THE SO-CALLED "TOMB OF QUEEN TIY"

In 1907, archaeologists working with funds provided by the American philanthropist Theodore Davis uncovered a small, undecorated rock-cut tomb (no. 55) in the Valley of the Kings at Thebes. The tomb furniture was scanty and in bad condition and bore all the marks of being hastily assembled. The remains were found of a gold-covered shrine which, according to the inscriptions, was made by Akhenaten for his mother, Queen Tiy, and Davis therefore assumed that the tomb belonged to Queen Tiy. Among the rubble on the floor of this unfinished tomb was a damaged coffin containing a mummy. Unfortunately, thanks to the depradations of thieves and the effects of water seeping into it at some time, the mummy had been reduced to a skeleton.

Cartouche of Akhenaten

This skeleton was examined and pronounced to be that of a female, presumably Queen Tiy, but a little later the body was examined by Sir Grafton Elliot Smith, who was then Professor of Anatomy in Cairo, and he announced that the bones were those of a man. These pitiful remains then became the subject of a lively controversy that raged on and off until recently.

Once Elliot Smith had pronounced the bones to be those of a male, it was immediately assumed by some that the body belonged to the heretic Pharaoh Akhenaten. After his death Akhenaten's very name became anathema to the orthodox priests of Amen-Re, and the heretic's name was destroyed on all his monuments. Nothing would be more likely than that the Pharaoh's enemies would also try to destroy his corpse, thus, in Egyptian eyes, destroying his soul as well. Those who thought the body in Tomb 55 belonged to Akhenaten suggested that it had been saved from the priests of Amen-Re by a few loyal followers, brought to Thebes, and buried secretly with a few hastily assembled pieces of tomb furniture.

Vengeance of Amen-Re

79

One drawback to this theory was that the bones appeared to belong to a man who had died in his mid-twenties. Either it had to be assumed that Akhenaten came to the throne as a precocious child, put forward his religious reforms, and died before he was thirty, or the body was not his. A second school of thought therefore developed, suggesting the body was that of either Smenkhkare or Tutankhamen, Akhenaten's two successors. The discovery of Tutankhamen's tomb removed one of these candidates from the list, so from then on it was a straight choice between Akhenaten and Smenkhkare.

⊬ The "Akhenaten school" came up with a very plausible explanation about the supposed age of the body. To judge from his statues, Akhenaten may well have suffered from some disease. Could he have suffered from an ailment which is known to alter the structure of the bones, thus making it difficult to determine the age of the body at death? If so, Akhenaten may have been about forty at his death, but his bones would still resemble those of a much younger man.

While the pathologists argued over the skeleton, the archaeologists and the philologists re-examined the coffin and its inscriptions. It became clear that the coffin had been intended for a woman, for the coffins of men and women were of different styles, and this one had originally been made in the woman's style, though it had been altered for a royal male occupant.

The inscriptions told the same story. The dedications had originally been for a woman, most probably Meritaten, eldest daughter of Akhenaten and wife of Smenkhkare. It was already known that Smenkhkare had died unexpectedly as a young man, so it is quite possible that his funeral equipment was not ready and that he was buried in a coffin, originally made for his wife, but hastily altered to meet his needs.

In December, 1963, the remains, then in the Cairo Museum, were examined by a team of eminent British and Egyptian doctors and professors. The body was then transferred to the Qasr el-Aini Hospital in Cairo, where it underwent a series of extensive anatomical and radiological tests. The results of the tests were as follows. The remains were undoubtedly those of a male, who had died aged certainly less than twenty-five. At the time of death he had been just about 1·7 metres in height. He bore a very close resemblance in facial appearance to

Tutankhamen, and it would seem most likely that they were brothers, or at least very closely related. Though some of the physical characteristics were slightly effeminate, there was no sign of the marked physical peculiarities displayed by statues of Akhenaten.

When all this information is taken into consideration, it would seem that the body from Tomb 55 has now finally been identified as that of Smenkhkare. May he rest in peace.

CHAPTER FIVE

Archaeological Problems

After spending several hours wandering around some of the world's great collections of Egyptian antiquities, such as are to be found in the Cairo Museum, the British Museum in London, the Louvre in Paris, the Metropolitan Museum of Art in New York, and many others, the visitor may very well begin to wonder whether there can possibly be anything left in the ground to be found by the modern archaeologists! Yet, year after year, the work goes on, lost monuments are discovered, and new objects swell the world's collections of antiquities. It seems that there is still a lot for future archaeologists to find, and there are certainly many exciting problems left to be solved. There are, in fact, so many problems that need solving that it has been extremely difficult to choose a few examples to talk about here. The following have been chosen because they are problems which must be solved by archaeologists rather than by linguists, and some of them call for co-operation between Egyptologists and scholars in other branches of archaeology in Palestine, Mesopotamia, Arabia, and Africa.

THE DATING OF THE PREDYNASTIC CULTURES OF EGYPT AND THE "DYNASTIC RACE"

This is really two separate problems, but as they are closely linked, they can be dealt with together. They concern the very early times in Egypt, before the unification of the two kingdoms under one ruler. As this was before the introduction of writing, there are no documents to help the investigation.

Archaeologists have so far discovered four different cultures that developed in Egypt before 3100 B.C. A village called Merimdah was excavated in the south western corner of the Delta, where a small community of early farmers was found to have lived. These people had several types of domesticated animals, and they cultivated grain, which they stored in silos of

A pot of the Gerzean Period showing a boat

mud-covered baskets. Their huts were fragile affairs, their tools were made of flint, and they had not discovered the use of metals. They could make pottery, but it was a rough ware, shaped by hand without a potter's wheel. As ornaments, they had beads of bone and shell and bracelets of ivory, and the presence of spindle whorls shows that they could weave. The date of the Merimdah settlement is unknown, but it may be the earliest of the Predynastic cultures so far discovered in Egypt.

On the valley edges in Upper Egypt three cultures have been identified, called Badarian, Amratian, and Gerzean after the sites where their remains were first discovered. It seems generally agreed that these cultures flourished one after another, but their exact relationship one to another has been disputed. Each of the three cultures had its own distinctive forms of pottery. The Badarians produced some wonderfully fine red burnished ware; Amratian pottery was also red, but decorated with cream-coloured patterns and figures of hippopotami and people; the Gerzean pottery was buff-coloured and decorated in red with lively scenes of boats, animals, birds, and people. Though flint tools were used, some of them beautifully

Predynastic cultures

83

made, from Badarian times onward the use of copper and gold was known. Some glazed beads show that the Badarians either had learned how to glaze or were importing these beads from somewhere. Basketry, mat-making, and weaving were among their accomplishments, and by the end of the Gerzean period they were producing exquisite vessels in all types of stone and were building large structures of mud bricks. Small slate palettes still showing traces of malachite indicate that eye paint was in use from Badarian times onward.

Not enough work has yet been done to establish what connections they had with their near neighbours, the Nubians and the Libyans. An even more pressing problem is to find out how widely each culture spread over Egypt, roughly how long each one lasted, and whether the cultures of Upper and Lower Egypt were very different from one another. To find out these things a series of digs will eventually have to be made throughout the Nile Valley, and especially in the Delta, about which very little is known for this early period. Unfortunately, excavations on such a large scale would cost a great deal of money. During such investigations samples would have to be taken from each site for carbon 14 analysis, and this, too, would be expensive. It has been pointed out in Chapter Four that this process is not yet perfect, but carbon 14 dates would help archaeologists to work out the relationships of the Predynastic cultures by revealing roughly when each site was occupied.

During the very earliest period of its history Egypt was divided into many small, independent communities, each ruled by its own petty chieftain and each under the protection of its own local divinity. Life was hard and insecure, dependent on the bounty of the Nile, but the soil of Egypt is very fertile. Gradually wealth and population increased, and the small communities joined one with another, by conquest and alliance, until there were just two kings, one in Upper Egypt, wearing the White Crown, and one in Lower Egypt, wearing the Red Crown. Then the King of Upper Egypt (tradition says his name was Menes) conquered his rival and united the Two Lands under his rule. To the very end of Pharaonic history, Egypt was always regarded as two lands, united in the person of their joint ruler, and each department of government was divided into two, one for Upper and one for Lower Egypt.

Just before the unification of the Two Lands by Menes,

The Unification of the Two Lands

(*opposite*) A Predynastic mace head showing King Scorpion

Egyptian culture seems to have developed at a greatly accelerated rate. Society became rich, and a high degree of skill and sophistication is shown in the objects produced by the craftsmen. Monumental buildings in mud brick were erected, and writing was introduced. At the same time there is also evidence that strong Mesopotamian influence was being felt in Egypt. For example, the brick monuments were built in a style of architecture known as the "palace façade" style, which had already been developed in Mesopotamia. Writing appears fully developed in Egypt, whereas in Mesopotamia a long history of experimentation in this art can be traced, and it has been suggested, therefore, that writing was introduced into Egypt from Mesopotamia. Products of Mesopotamia – for example, the cylinder seal, that most characteristic of all Mesopotamian artifacts – make a sudden appearance in Egypt, as do Mesopotamian art motifs like the hero overcoming two wild beasts. Mesopotamia therefore clearly offered an exciting stimulus to the already expanding Egyptian culture in both the technical and artistic fields.

The "Dynastic Race" The big problem is to decide whether this influence was the result of direct trade between the two areas, or the intervention of a third party, as yet unidentified, or whether, as some authorities suggest, there was an invasion of Egypt by what they call the "Dynastic Race" – a race of warriors who conquered the native peasants and became a ruling élite of warriors, priests, and kings. Only the excavation of a great deal of material of the right period can provide an answer to this puzzle. If there *was* an invasion in the Late Predynastic Period, where exactly did this come from and by what route did the conquerors arrive? Did they march in overland, following the Fertile Crescent down through Palestine? Or did they come by ships down the Persian Gulf, along the coast of Arabia, and so up the Red Sea coast, and then land and cross the desert through the Wadi Hammamat? There are certainly pictures of boats on pottery and in tombs of this period, but they may have been only for use on the river. Even if the influence of Mesopotamia was not brought by warriors but by peaceful traders, the problem of their route is still the same. The whole question of trade at this period needs to be studied. To take but one puzzling example, in the Late Predynastic Period the Egyptians were making beads out of lapis lazuli. The nearest known source of this semi-precious stone to Egypt is Afghanistan, over two thousand miles away! How did it get to Egypt? How many pairs of hands did it pass through? It is only by very careful excavation of both the land route and the coast along the sea route that the answer to this problem is going to be found, and a great deal of co-operation by specialists in several different archaeological fields may be needed before a satisfactory solution is reached.

WHERE WAS THE LAND OF PUNT?

From the very early days one of the things considered by the Egyptians to be most necessary for the correct worship of the gods was incense, and the land of Punt seems to have been the source of Egypt's best incense. Inscriptions show that at least from the Fifth Dynasty, and in fact probably much earlier, the Egyptians were going to Punt and bringing back incense. These expeditions must have been fairly regular occurrences, though each Pharaoh always claimed that nothing like it had ever been done before. Though incense is the product most usually connected with Punt, the Egyptians brought back other products, as well. Toward the end of the Sixth Dynasty, Pepi II, then only a boy of about eight, wrote to Harkhuf, Prince of Aswan. Harkhuf, who, as prince of this province, which contained the First Cataract, bore the colourful title of "Keeper of the Door of the South", had made several trading expeditions up river. Pepi's letter expresses delight because Harkhuf was bringing him home a dancing dwarf like the one who had been brought from Punt to a previous king.

Thanks to tomb paintings of various periods and to the great sculptured scenes of the expedition that went to Punt in year nine of the reign of Queen Hatshepsut and was recorded on the walls of her temple at Deir el Bahari, quite a lot is known about this trade. To reach the land of Punt, the Egyptians seem to have crossed the Eastern Desert, probably via the Wadi Hammamat, till they reached the coast, where they took ship and sailed south down the Red Sea. Hatshepsut shows her expedition setting out from the capital, Thebes, under the leadership of the chief treasurer, Nehsi, and his reception at a Puntite village, where the trading took place under the eyes of the chieftain of the Puntites and his grotesquely ugly wife. Former expeditions had simply brought home incense resin, but it was Nehsi's task to bring back living myrrh trees to be

Hatshepsut's great expedition

87

The Chieftain of Punt and his wife

planted in Egypt. The Puntite chief seems to have been very pleased with the goods which Nehsi brought him from Egypt, for the Egyptian ships are shown returning home loaded not only with myrrh trees, but also with myrrh resin, ebony, ivory, gold, cinnamon wood, eye paint, monkeys, dogs, and panther skins. A Theban tomb painting of the Eighteenth Dynasty shows another trading venture with Punt, and on this occasion the Puntites are shown sailing small rafts loaded with merchandise.

All the evidence indicates that the Egyptians regarded the trade with Punt as being very valuable, and yet it is still not certain where Punt was situated. The two locations considered by authorities to be the most likely sites of Punt are southern Arabia and Somaliland. To judge from the products brought from Punt, Somaliland is considered to be the more likely location, but if southern Arabia was the ancient Punt, then those products which were not naturally found there might have been brought to the trading post from elsewhere for re-export. Only thorough excavations of both areas, to find Egyptian objects and to identify trading centres, will settle the controversy.

WHO WERE THE HYKSOS?

After the unification of the Two Lands by Menes, Egypt enjoyed an era of great prosperity. This was the period of the Old Kingdom, when the great pyramids of the Gizah group were built and some of the most superb pieces of portrait sculpture of all times were produced. For centuries Egypt was rich and her frontiers were secure, but then came a period of weakness and civil strife when foreigners infiltrated the Delta. After a while, a family of strong rulers emerged in Thebes and eventually swept north under the leadership of Nebhepetre Mentuhotep (see Chapter Three), uniting Egypt under one ruler once more. Under the new rulers of the Middle Kingdom, Egypt enjoyed one of the greatest periods in her history. But, just as at the end of the Old Kingdom, the strong, centralized power of the monarchy gradually weakened, and in the Thirteenth Dynasty Egypt drifted into another period of

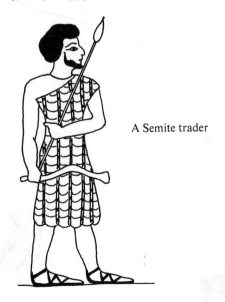

A Semite trader

decline, until in about 1670 B.C., traditionally in the reign of the Pharaoh Dudimose, Egypt suffered the humiliation of being invaded from the north east by those whom she had always referred to contemptuously as "Asiatics" and "miserable sand-dwellers". At first these Asiatics probably came as peaceful traders, like those shown in one of the tombs at Beni Hasan. Some may have come looking for fresh pastures for their herds. "They said moreover unto Pharaoh, For to sojourn in the land are we come; for thy servants have no pasture for their flocks; for the famine is sore in the land of Canaan: now therefore, we pray thee, let thy servants dwell in the land of Goshen" (Genesis 47:4). A papyrus now in the Brooklyn Museum shows that many Asiatics were house slaves in Egypt at this time. "And the Midianites sold him into Egypt unto Potiphar, an officer of Pharaoh's, and captain of the guard" (Genesis 37:36). If the description of affairs in Egypt has invited comparison with the Biblical story of Joseph and his brethren, it is hardly to be wondered at, for it would have been about this time, the Second Intermediate Period as it is called in Egyptian history, that Joseph, Jacob, and their families settled in Egypt.

They may have drifted peacefully into Egypt at first, but later the Asiatics, finding no central authority powerful enough to stop them, came in in larger numbers than before and took over the government in the Delta. It may be that besides the traders, servants, and herdsmen mentioned above, there was also a more aggressive element among the immigrants – a number of warriors, perhaps fighting from horse-drawn chariots, which were hitherto unknown in Egypt.

These Asiatics are known to us as the Hyksos, a name once thought to mean "shepherd kings" but which is now recognized to be a corruption of two Egyptian words meaning "chieftains of hill countries" or "rulers of foreign lands".

Hyksos rule   The Egyptians never forgot this shattering blow to their pride and later accused the Hyksos of all sorts of impiety and atrocities. Hatshepsut, for example, in her inscription in her temple at Speos Artemidos, speaks of buildings being in ruins after Hyksos depredations and claims that the Asiatics ruled in ignorance of Re (the Egyptian sun god), while Manetho accuses them of burning cities, destroying temples, murdering citizens, and carrying off women and children into slavery. Probably

90   such acts were committed during the establishment of Hyksos

rule in the Delta region. Such a takeover would hardly have been entirely peaceful. Nevertheless, our evidence shows that once they were established, the Hyksos adopted Egyptian manners, customs, art forms, names, titles, writing, and religion. They became so thoroughly Egyptianized, in fact, that in the present state of our knowledge it is virtually impossible to find anything that is typically Hyksos. Even the scarabs, which were produced in such great numbers at this time, already had a long history in Egypt. However, recent Austrian excavations in the Delta have revealed, on one site at any rate, some very un-Egyptian-looking burials with which horses are connected. There is literary evidence to show that sometimes, at least, the native Egyptian rulers, who precariously maintained an independent southern state based at Thebes, were on such good terms with the Hyksos kings, who ruled the Delta from their capital of Avaris, that the Thebans were allowed to pasture their cattle in the Delta.

A scarab

The "war of liberation" began, according to one Egyptian story, when a Hyksos king, Apophis, complained to Sekenenre, the ruler of the South, that the roaring of the hippopotami in a pool in Thebes kept him awake in Avaris, several hundred miles away! This must rank as one of the strangest excuses for making war of all times. It is an interesting footnote to this story that the mummy of King Sekenenre has been found, and it has several horrible head wounds. It is therefore possible that he fell in battle against the Hyksos. Finally, in about 1567 B.C., the Hyksos were defeated by Kamose, the son of Sekenenre, and the victorious Egyptians swept through the Delta and on to magnificent conquests in Palestine and Syria.

"War of Liberation"

It is still not known just exactly who the Hyksos were. They certainly contained a Semitic element, to judge by some of their names, but there were possibly other elements, as well, though who they were is not clear. Nor is it clear just how close were the contacts that they maintained with Palestine, though we know from an inscription of Kamose that Apophis was in league with the King of Kush (Kush covered part of Nubia and part of the Sudan). What is really needed is a series of excavations in the Delta, especially in the eastern Delta, to try to identify more objects that could belong to the period of Hyksos domination. These must then be compared with material from the valley to see how far their influence extended, and with

91

material from Palestine to find out how closely the two areas were linked.

THE END OF THE AMARNA AGE

With the expulsion of the Hyksos and the beginning of the Eighteenth Dynasty, Egypt entered one of the most glorious periods of her long history. A dynasty of warrior Pharaohs led their armies out of Egypt on a long series of conquests, marching north through Palestine and Syria right to the banks of the river Euphrates, and south through Nubia and Kush to the Fifth Cataract of the Nile. Tribute from the conquered territories flowed into Egypt, and the rulers of Crete and the Mediterranean islands sent presents, making the Pharaohs the greatest and richest kings in the Near East. Kings wrote begging letters to Egypt. The king of the Mitanni of northern Syria, for example, asked that "his brother" of Egypt should send him gold in very great quantities, because gold in Egypt was as common as dust.

At the height of all this power and prosperity, the then Pharaoh, Amenhotep III, died and was succeeded by his son, Amenhotep IV, who changed his name to Akhenaten. The character of this Pharaoh has fascinated historians for many years. He has been called everything from prophet, idealist, and reformer to religious maniac, weakling, and madman. Perhaps the true nature of this enigmatic man will never be revealed, but people will continue to study his actions and draw their own conclusions. Akhenaten worshipped the god Aten, whose visible manifestation was the sun's disk. But instead of simply making his cult fashionable, as other kings had done when they favoured a particular deity, by heaping wealth on the god's priests and *"Heretic"* building him huge temples, Akhenaten tried to suppress the *Pharaoh* worship of all the other Egyptian gods and make the Aten supreme. He abandoned Thebes, the capital of his forefathers and the home of the state god, the ram-headed Amen-Re, and built a new capital city for himself and his god at the place now known as Tell el Amarna. Akhenaten called his new city Akhetaten, "The Horizon of the Aten", and here he lived with his family, his priests, and his courtiers and worshipped the Aten, ordering the worship of all other gods to cease and even having the names of the proscribed deities blocked out on all
92　the monuments of Egypt.

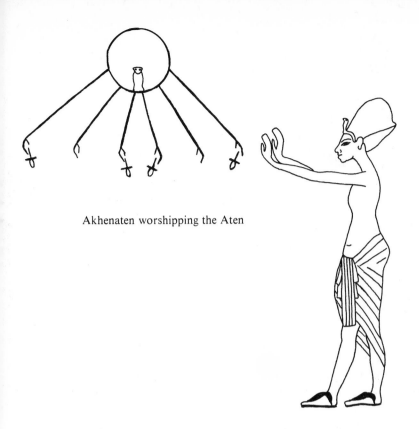

Akhenaten worshipping the Aten

The portraits of Akhenaten which have survived are frankly ugly. They show him as having an elongated head held forward on a thin neck. The face is narrow, the lips are thick, and the body seems to have been hollow-chested, with a paunch, wide thighs, and skinny calves. Thanks to her beautiful portrait bust, which archaeologists found in the ruined studio of the master sculptor Tuthmosis, Akhenaten's wife, Nefertiti, has become *Queen* one of the most famous women of the ancient world. If the *Nefertiti* portrait is a true likeness, then her name, which means "the beautiful woman comes", was very apt. On the monuments at Amarna the king and queen are shown as a devoted couple, surrounded by their six daughters, Nefertiti's sister, Akhenaten's mother, Queen Tiy, and his sister, Beketaten.

In the court at "The Horizon of Aten", Akhenaten might be able to propagate his new theology, but elsewhere the forces of reaction were too strong for him. Even in the workmen's village at Amarna (see Chapter Three), plenty of amulets were found that showed that the inhabitants were still faithful to the old divinities. After a reign of some seventeen years Akhenaten died. His chosen successor and son-in-law, Smenkhkare, died roughly at the same time, so Akhenaten was replaced on the throne by a child of nine, another of his sons-in-law, called Tutankhaten. This boy was himself destined to rule only about nine years. During his reign the court moved back to Thebes, the old gods were reinstated, the Aten was abandoned, and the Pharaoh changed his name to Tutankhamen. Tutankhamen was succeeded in his turn by Ay, a courtier, and then by the general of the armies, Horemheb, during whose reign Akhenaten came to be regarded as an accursed heretic whose memory was ruthlessly persecuted.

The triumph of Amen-Re

Such, very briefly, was the dramatic end of the fascinating Amarna Age. But as so often happens, history has left many tantalizing loose ends to be tied by the archaeologist. Here, briefly, are a few of them.

(*a*) What happened to the body of Akhenaten? Was he really buried in the tomb he had had prepared for himself in the cliff of a wadi in the desert east of Amarna? If so, this was later looted, and the body was presumably destroyed. Or did his loyal followers, fearing the revenge of the priests of Amen-Re, secretly lay their master to rest elsewhere? A thorough investigation of material from the looted royal tomb is now under way and may provide answers to these and other questions.

(*b*) What happened to Nefertiti? The excavators of Amarna suggest that, from the evidence they gathered, Nefertiti may have moved into a separate palace in about the twelfth year of the reign. If so, why? Did she, though this is only speculation, realize that her husband's activities were costing Egypt her empire in Asia and causing dissention at home, and so quarrel with him over future policy? Certainly her name is replaced on buildings by that of her eldest daughter, Meritaten. Was she already dead before Tutankhamen came to the throne? If not, when did she die, and where was she buried? So far, no objects have come to light which could be thought to be part of the queen's funerary equipment. Does this mean that the final resting place of "the King's Great Wife, his beloved, the Lady of the Two Lands, Nefer-neferu-Aten Nefertiti" has yet to be found?

94

Two of Akhenaten's daughters

(c) What happened to Nefertiti's daughters? Akhenaten and Nefertiti had six daughters. The second daughter, Meketaten, is known to have died as a girl, and there are pictures at Amarna showing the royal family grieving over the small corpse; but the eldest girl, Meritaten, grew up and married the king's chosen successor, Smenkhkare. Her husband and her father died at about the same time, and her subsequent fate is unknown. The third daughter's career is a little better documented. This girl, Ankhesenpaaten as she was called, may have married her own father at the end of his reign. There is an inscription from a building at Hermopolis which mentions Ankhesenpaaten and her daughter, Ankhesenpaaten the Younger, together with Akhenaten. The inscription is damaged, but some scholars have taken it to mean that Akhenaten married his daughter and had a child by her. There is ample evidence to 95 show that many of the Pharaohs married their sisters, but marriages between father and daughter seem to have been very rare indeed; in fact, only one other father–daughter marriage is known, and all scholars do not agree about that, either. This is the possible marriage between Amenhotep III and his daughter, Sitamen.

After the death of Akhenaten, Ankhesenpaaten changed her name to Ankhesenamen, because all mention of the Aten was now forbidden, and she married Tutankhamen. The representations of her in the tomb of Tutankhamen show her as a beautiful but fragile creature. At the time of his death Ankhesenamen was still only in her early twenties. She was heiress presumptive to the throne of Egypt, and whoever married her would be the next Pharaoh. Chance is sometimes kind to the archaeologist. Two letters have been discovered which Ankhesenamen wrote to Shubilulliuma, the king of the Hittites, beseeching him to send one of his sons to be her husband, because there was no one in Egypt of high enough rank to marry her, and she did not want to marry a servant.

Cartouche of
Ankhesenamen

*Palace
intrigue*

For her dramatic intrigue with the old enemy of Egypt the desperate widow only had the seventy days during which Tutankhamen's body was being mummified. It was not enough. The paintings in the tomb of Tutankhamen show that his funeral ceremony was conducted by the new Pharaoh, Ay. A ring has been found bearing the names of Ay and Ankhesenamen, linked together in royal cartouches, suggesting that the queen had been forced to marry her elderly servant, after all. After that, nothing. If a Hittite prince did set out for Egypt, he was never allowed to reach the frontier, and in the tomb of Ay, the queen at his side is not Ankhesenamen but the woman he had married years before, who had been Nefertiti's nurse. Some future find may reveal what happened to Ankhesenamen and her three young sisters, but until then the fate of these young women is unknown and, one suspects, tragic. It would not be the first or the last time that innocent, but politically dangerous people, have been quietly "removed".

"WHERE, OH WHERE, IS IMHOTEP?"
So one archaeologist wrote in a letter after years searching for the tomb of one of Egypt's greatest men. From a statue base in the Cairo Museum, we know that Imhotep was "Seal Bearer",

96

which was an important administrative post, at the court of Zoser, the great Pharaoh of the Third Dynasty. Tradition says that Imhotep was a brilliant man of many and varied talents, who has been referred to as the Leonardo da Vinci of the ancient world. Besides being a government official, Imhotep was a sage, a doctor, and an architect. He is best remembered as the architect who designed Zoser's tomb, the Step Pyramid at Sakkara, which was the first pyramid to be built.

"Leonardo of the Ancient World"

Until the reign of Zoser, kings had been buried in mastaba tombs, but Imhotep enlarged Zoser's mastaba to a great size and then put a whole series of stone "steps" on top. The reason for this drastic change of plan has never been fully ascertained, but one plausible suggestion is that he was trying to build a ladder by which the god-king could climb to the sky. It is certainly true that if you are lucky, on a winter's day at Gizah when there is plenty of cloud about, you can see the sun's rays streaming through the clouds and forming a pyramid in sunbeams. Perhaps the Egyptians were trying to preserve this rather unusual ladder to the sky in stone.

After his death, Imhotep's reputation for wisdom grew until finally, in the Late Period, he was deified as the patron of scribes and the god of medicine. The Greeks, who settled in Egypt in the Late Period, identified Imhotep with their own god of medicine, Aesculapius. At this time a great temple was built and dedicated to Imhotep–Aesculapius on the traditional site of his tomb. This was the famous Aesculapium, and pilgrims flocked to it, not only from all over Egypt, but from the whole of the Mediterranean area. The sick spent the night sleeping in the temple, and there they had visions of the god in dreams and their maladies were cured by the priests.

When Egypt became Christian, the old religion fell into disfavour, and finally all pagan shrines were attacked and destroyed. Inevitably such a famous shrine as the Aesculapium attracted the particular attention of the fanatics, and its very site disappeared from the map.

Christian fanatics

The most likely location of Imhotep's tomb and the temple which stood above it is the necropolis of the nobles of the Third Dynasty, which is situated at Sakkara, near the Step Pyramid. During the last hundred years or so, many famous archaeologists have searched the desert at Sakkara for some trace of this great temple and tomb. In October, 1964, an expedition

Imhotep

A sacred ibis, its mummy, and pottery coffin

sponsored by the Egyptian Exploration Society of London began work at Sakkara under the direction of Professor W. B. Emery of University College, London, searching for the tomb of Imhotep. Though this has not, as yet, come to light, another ancient temple has been uncovered which bears eloquent testimony to the fury of the early Christian fanatics. The building was razed to the ground, documents were torn up and scattered to the four winds, and sacred statues were smashed and the pieces scattered in all directions.

Two of Egypt's sacred animals, the ibis and the Apis bull, became particularly associated with Imhotep, and besides the remains of the temple and its furniture, the Egypt Exploration Society's excavation has revealed a vast network of underground galleries in which were buried ibises, hawks, baboons, and cows, the mothers of the sacred bulls of Apis, which were buried in the nearby Serapeum. These animals were buried as if they were human mummies, enclosed in layers of intricately wrapped bandages. There were literally hundreds of thousands of mummified ibises, all wrapped and buried, each in its own pottery container. All these finds are encouraging signs that the Aesculapium may be near, but as yet the elusive Imhotep has not been found.

Animal burials

99

A TOWN SITE

The foregoing examples are of problems connected with specific people and areas. Mention must now be made of a more general but nevertheless very important task for the archaeologist. It was pointed out in Chapter Two that a great deal of our information about the ancient Egyptians comes from their tombs and that little work has been done on their settlements, because so many have been built over by modern villages and towns. No matter what the difficulties, and these are considerable, the time has now come when a concerted effort must be made to excavate several settlement sites up and down the country. The sites need not be large ones; in fact, it would be much easier if they were comparatively modest in size. What is of vital importance is that objects and pottery of daily use can be found in position and that stratified material can be examined. The cost of such a programme would, of course, be high, and it would take a long time to complete, but the knowledge gained would be of inestimable value.

For Further Reading

The following books provide a starting point for further study.

For the general reader:

G. Belzoni, *Narrative of the Operations* (Murray, London)
M. Chubb, *Nefertiti Lived Here* (T. Y. Crowell Co., New York)
L. Cottrell, *Life Under the Pharaohs* (Evans, London)
L. Cottrell, *The Warrior Pharaohs* (Putnam's, New York)
Steven Frimmer, *The Stone That Spoke* (Putnam's, New York)
C. F. Nims, *Thebes of the Pharaohs* (Elek, London)
C. Desroches Noblecourt, *Tutankhamen* (Thames & Hudson, London)
Jon Manchip White, *Everyday Life in Ancient Egypt* (Putnam's, New York)
William Wise, *The Two Reigns of Tutankhamen* (Putnam's, New York)

For those who wish to go deeper:

C. Aldred, *Ancient Egyptian Art* (A. Tiranti Ltd, London)
I. E. S. Edwards, *The Pyramids of Egypt* (Penguin Books, London)
W. B. Emery, *Archaic Egypt* (Penguin Books, London)
W. B. Emery, *Egypt in Nubia* (Hutchinson, London)
A. H. Gardiner, *Egypt of the Pharaohs* (Clarendon Press, Oxford)
W. C. Hayes, *The Scepter of Egypt* (Harper [Harvard University Press], New York)
J. B. Pritchard, *Ancient Near Eastern Texts* (Princeton University Press, Princeton)
J. A. Wilson, *The Burden of Egypt* (Chicago University Press, Chicago)
H. E. Winlock, *The Rise and Fall of the Middle Kingdom in Thebes* (Macmillan, New York)

For those who wish to start serious study:

The Cambridge Ancient History volumes (Cambridge University Press, Cambridge)
The Journal of Egyptian Archaeology (Egypt Exploration Society, London)

109

Excavation Reports – these will be found in libraries under the names of the authors. The reader may like to begin with the following:

H. Carter, *The Tomb of Tutankhamen* (Cassell, London)

W. B. Emery, *Great Tombs of the First Dynasty* (Government Press, Cairo)

E. Naville, *The Eleventh Dynasty Temple at Deir el Bahari.* Memoirs of the Egypt Exploration Fund, London

P. E. Newberry, *The Rock Tombs of Beni Hasan.* Memoirs of the Egypt Exploration Fund, London

J. D. S. Pendlebury, *Tell el Amarna* (Lovat Dickson & Thompson, London)

W. M. Flinders Petrie, *Royal Tombs of the First and Second Dynasties.* Memoirs of the Egypt Exploration Fund, London

H. E. Winlock, *The Treasure of el Lahun* (Metropolitan Museum of Art, New York)

Index

111